ONLY ONE SHOT

ONLY ONE SHOT

Creating a Disciplined, Defined and

Loving Environment

for Junior Golfers

V.J. Trolio

Editor / Susan Schadt

SUSAN SCHADT PRESS

ONE ONE SHOT

Published in 2025 by

Susan Schadt Press, LLC

New Orleans

© VJ Trolio

Designed by Reid Mitchell

All rights reserved. No part of this publication may be reproduced, stored in any retrieval system or transmitted in any form or by any means, electronic, mechanical, photocopying or otherwise, without prior permission in writing from the publisher.

Although every precaution has been taken to verify the accuracy of the information contained herein, the author and publisher assume no responsibility for any errors or omissions. No liability is assumed for damages that may result from the use of information contained within.

Library of Congress Control Number 2019901841

ISBN 979-89874780-6-6

TABLE OF CONTENTS

PREFACE vii

1. DRIVEN 1
2. Who Are You? 11
3. 1st JTG 28
4. UNDERWATER BB STACKING 60
5. OUR INNER DUMMIES 86
6. THE BEGINING 103
7. ¿HABLAS EL IDIOMA DE LOS CAMPEONES? 122
8. HUH? 133
9. The Rise 144
10. "I AM GOING TO DISNEY WORLD" 160
11. REVIVED 176
12. RANKINGS 197
13. STORIES 210
14. A THING OR TWO ABOUT PRACTICE 216
15. EPILOGUE 227

PREFACE

Everyone who knows me knows that I love music. I can't sing. I can't play an instrument. To my knowledge there has never been a Trolio that could; but that doesn't prevent me from playing it all day long.

If you are like me, competition and life are very similar. Both have a tempo and a timing to them. Both present a tone that changes and flows. If the voice is the "orchestra of the heart" then competition reveals the "character of our heart."

If you think like me, much of life can be summed up by our character, our words, and how we go about presenting that to those around us. A person of good character with wise words, that are presented to us at the right time with the correct tone can be life changing.

Elite competitors who are tough, gritty, and healthy are mentored by individuals with this sort of knowledge. There is no one more important to the development of an athlete than their parents. Laying the responsibility in the lap of a coach or mentor will not get the job done.

This book was written to present a process to create a discipline, defined, and honest environment for an athlete. This book was written so a parent and athlete could see past today and into tomorrow. This book was written so young athletes win on the course and off the golf course.

It is not meant to be THE guide but instead a base that a philosophy could be built around. It is not meant to be a story, although you will find one here. The story is that of a GUIDE that did in fact create a HERO. But as with all things, seeing behind the scenes allows us to learn so much more.

Although PGA Professionals win awards and accolades for their ability to teach and coach golf, they are a small part of the team. Parents are the most important part of the team, they are the GUIDE and the HERO, guiding the mindset their golfers will carry for the rest of their lives.

Ultimately it should be the athletes' intention to win; but should that be the emphasis of the parents?
Proverbs 3:5-6

All heroes need a guide and sometimes that guide has **ONLY ONE SHOT.**

This book is dedicated to you, the guide,

And to the five guides who we all believe are heroes:

Linda Meeks
Janie Gallagher
Lynda Trolio
Cissye Gallagher
Allison Trolio

1

DRIVEN

Many parents are driven to remove obstacles in the way of their offspring. Sometimes obstacles are physical, sometimes mental. sometimes obstacles simply stem from a lack of knowledge. Whether the situation involves poor grades, a reading comprehension problem, a lack of confidence or even the wrong golf equipment—nearly all of us share a sense of urgency for our children.

There are two approaches for how parents deal with this sense of urgency. One approach is consistent with individuals being in total control of their own destiny. The other approach is consistent with the thought that individuals are not in total control of their own destiny. The first camp suggests that we make decisions and perform actions in order to sharpen ourselves. The later camp suggests that we make decisions and perform actions to be sharpened. The first approach is "self-grooming" and the second is a "we are being groomed" approach.

Personally, I believe in the "we are being groomed" approach. One of the many ways I am being groomed has always been through the game of golf. My passion for this game has taken me many places for many different reasons. In the beginning it was a place mostly of independence and fun. Later the game took me to competitive places. Over the past decade the game has primarily taken me to places of learning and teaching. What amazes me is that the game of golf is still all of these places for me.

Of all the wonders that God has created, human beings stand atop the list. As a human race, century after century, we have been driven. I need to point out something obvious: **The communities of people I find *everywhere* are still DRIVEN**. Whether it is competing, sharing knowledge, teaching or learning, we all have an instinctual drive in common. We humans have always had this sense of drive. At one point we were hunters and gatherers and then we became explorers looking for new lands. Even when the accepted thinking was that the world was flat, humans were driven to sail out to where the sky met the water.

In the world we live in the seas, the moon and even distant planets have been discovered and visited by humans or their machines. We have conquered, destroyed, saved and given peace to countless millions. But what do we find ourselves doing in the current modern world? We are turning to our families and ourselves. We are turning inward.

Sports psychology did not exist one hundred years ago. The idea of the self-image arose in the 1950s and was clearly covered in Psycho-Cybernetics during the 1970s. Freud's theory of the id and Williams James's concept of positive thinking were focused on this newly discovered human drive—the drive to fix oneself. The simple reason sports psychology arose was that humans want better outcomes. You want a better body. You want to feel comfortable in a room. You want to be good public speaker. You want to finish first—on top of the heap.

Researchers have looked at the origin of sports. It seems that sports, from bowling to skeet shooting, stem from having our needs being met. Humans moved for centuries. If you wanted it, you had to go get it. We jumped, threw and climbed. All this movement turned into sport. Over the centuries as our race was graced with food, safety and shelter, our drives led to the multitude of sports that we now enjoy. In fact, humans actually pay to watch the best at the sports we love because they show us just how good a driven human can become.

The human drive works in a continuum. No matter where you find your problem, there is an answer. Not only is there an answer, there is an example of some other human that was driven to perfect that which you find wrong with yourself. You can pay them or their company to teach you how they were able to overcome the problem. Sadly, as we look for answers, many times the answers don't "take."

Here is a possible problem. The Driven Human is looking for ways to influence an outcome. The Driven Human is not looking for the knowledge of the process. Understanding the process into which we plug knowledge and answers is vital to being successful.

You should know that I am also a Driven Human. My passion centers mostly on the world of golf. For the past two decades I have taught, or rather given, people an incentive to become better at the sport called golf. What I have learned reminds me of a simple parable from Jesus found in Luke. The parable concerns a planted tree. After three seasons, the tree did not bear fruit. The owner of the property asked his gardener to pull up the tree. The gardener requested that the owner wait one more season so he could dig around the tree and replace some of the soil with fertilizer. If the tree does not bear fruit, then the gardener will take it down.

I only wish this were the case for all of us Driven Humans. We often see our child not producing and we immediately want to fix this poor outcome. So, what is your urgent obligation? Did it arise because you or your son or daughter did not perform well last week on the course? Did it arise because there was an episode in competition that somehow brought out a failure? Did it arise because of the performance of another athlete?

People walk into my golf shop all the time with problems with their golf games. They walk in with problems with their body. They walk in with problems with their brains. Trust me, these individuals are driven. The only problem is, they can't tell me their problem. Immediately the discussion (if I let them) turns to ball flight or scores. Immediately they jump to the outcome and want to know how to fix it!

Getting better at anything is a process of elimination and a process of defining how you eliminated the obstacle. But what eliminates the obstacle? Is it the mind? Is it the body? Is it the mechanics of the motion? As a general rule I ask these questions. In a sense I am saying, "OK tree, you aren't producing any fruit. I get that. But what makes up your soil?"

It is apparent to me that individuals drive themselves in different ways. It is also clear that changing or altering that drive so that it leads to better performance is handled quite differently among individuals. This difference is why there are essentially three forms of psychology: **Cognitive, Constraint** and **Behavioral**. While we lie awake driven to fix our children or ourselves and we come up with plans. These plans are all laid in the foundation of one of these areas of psychology.

Understand that we, as humans, rarely care until we are emotionally involved. Just go to a little league baseball game to understand what "being emotionally involved" looks like. For example, an eight-year-old girl steps into the batter's box.

- **Story One.** She hits a scorcher at the third baseman, and, to his father's dismay, the ball goes right between his feet. The runners on second and third score the tying and winning runs. The error by the third baseman helped decide the outcome. Now who do you think got scolded? Who do you think got the praise?

- **Story Two.** To her father's dismay, she looks at three straight strikes— the bat never leaving her shoulder. The pitcher's parents go bonkers. Her ineptitude strands the runners and the game is lost. Now whom do you think got the praise? Who do you think got scolded?

Let's put a similar example into a golf tournament.

- Story One. A young man is eight over par in his first twelve holes, but then makes six straight birdies to shoot 74. Is the parent angry or frustrated?

- Story Two. A young man is four under par through twelve holes, but finished with six straight bogies to shoot 74. Is the parent angry or frustrated?

Driven we are. Driven to heal, steal, help and sometimes destroy. Will our drive ever change? Has anyone changed it? Do we all think the same way? The answer to the last question is all around you. Ninety-five percent of the people do the losing. Five percent of the people do ninety-five percent of the winning. Essentially, ninety- five percent of us are castles made of sand. As long as the tide doesn't come in too far, we will be ok. But as the wind, rain and tide roll in, we falter.

Suppose preparation mattered more than the performance. That is, what if we cared more about the fertilizer around the tree than how much fruit it bore? What if our castles were made of stone rather than of sand? What if the process of building the castle was laid out so well that no matter how big the wave, we could recover?

I believe such a process can be built. I believe we can turn our drive toward being helpful on the golf course and other areas of our lives. I have seen it happen and I work to make it happen with everyone who walks in the door of my shop.

There is a reason I believe we can turn our drive toward being helpful. In twelve years I have been a part of approximately fifty state championships. I have been a part of two individuals making it to the semi-finals of USGA Championships and the only First Team All-American born in Mississippi. I have been a part of success on the Nationwide and PGA Tours. These people are not built differently from others. The difference is simple: their drive is anchored in things they can control. Those that do not bear as much fruit are generally more concerned with the fruit rather than the soil. If we can focus on the soil, the fruit will come.

I once did a Bible study with a group of friends and we read a John Eldridge book. There was a quote that went something like this "Every man must have three things: A battle to fight, an adventure to live, and a woman to save." That quote resonated with me as I thought, "Life is not that simple is it? Sometimes we find ourselves on the losing side of the battle. Sometimes our adventures are filled with anxiety. Sometimes our drives just push us (and our children) in the wrong direction."

Our body, while complex, needs only a few biological inputs. Our bodies need vitamins, protein, minerals, water and movement. The human brain is an intricate organ. One part of the brain, the limbic system, can really throw off this delicate machine. The limbic system appears to be primarily responsible for our emotional life and also has much to do with the formation of our memories.

Part of the limbic system is an organ called the hypothalamus, which is about the size of a thumb tip. The hypothalamus is responsible for regulating your hunger, thirst, response to pain, levels of pleasure, sexual satisfaction, anger and aggressive behavior. The hypothalamus is the source of our basic drives. When you wonder, "Why do I get so mad at my children on the baseball field?" you can go straight to your hypothalamus for the answer. The emotional state this little organ can create will blind the rest of our brain from rational choices all day long. It is the reason why when you say "no" another voice says you should have said "yes." Acclaimed writer Nigel Calder once said, "Had its functions been known in medieval times, the hypothalamus would no doubt have been designated the Devil's playground."

By the way, your hypothalamus is out there on the golf course with you. During a practice round, have you ever wondered why it is so easy to go for a par five in two, but during the tournament it is tough? Have you ever wondered why it is so easy for you to step up and make that four-foot putt on the practice green, but on the course your mind starts chattering to you? Have you ever wondered why tournament scores are higher than practice round scores? Sometimes there are no clear answers to questions like these.

These questions really center on personal growth and mindset. Dr. Clay Parker shared a concept that really helped me think about a possible way to guide parents to help their children as they grow. He laid the concept out like this:

Provider-Cop-Coach-Consultant

In the beginning we provide for and nurture our children. As they grow older, we become their cop: i.e., "Don't touch the stove!" Later, as they reach their teen years, children want a coach. The parent must become a coach because children in this stage desire "freedom" and a coach must "trust." If a parent is being a cop during this stage, however, the parent can stifle freedom by being commanding. As our children mature and set out on a life for themselves, they want a wise consultant. They have been coached long enough; now they only require help in

When I begin to discuss a "Routine" with a junior golfer, it is important for me to understand where both the junior golfer and their parents are from a basic mind-set perspective. Are the parents playing "cop" to their thirteen-year-old child? While we were all created similar in terms of biological parts like brains, muscles, bones, tendons and ligaments, we definitely are not all be raised the same way. The drive of parents has a tremendously positive (or negative) effect on their children. Generally, the outcome of this drive is mediocrity. Occasionally the outcome of this drive is greatness.

If I were to list some ways for anyone (including your children) to stay on the road to mediocrity, the list would include:

- Eat pasteurized foods.

- Drink a lot of sugar-loaded sodas.

- Limit your movement to video games, television, computers and smart phones.

- Let your brain rule you.

- Give into every indulgence.

- If you feel a need to do it, then do it.

- Be completely outcome oriented.
- Forget the process.
- Live for the moment.

If I were to list some ways to help anyone (including your children) be great, the list would include:

- Eat natural foods.
- Drink a lot of water.
- Begin your day with movement.
- Sustain movement through what we commonly call "exercise" every day.
- Define your goals.
- Ignore any impulse that does not fit into your goals.
- Use emotion on only what you can control.
- Be completely process oriented.
- Forget the outcome.
- Live life over the long run.

The concept that "one day you will get to a crossroad in your life and you must make the right decision" is false. Every single day is a crossroad in our lives. Every single day matters.

Take a stroll with us. Along the way you will be forced to build your philosophy. If you regret some of the things you have done in the past, let go of them. We can't go back and take a different path. After all, maybe that is the reason you found this book.

2

Who Are You?

Are some children more talented than others? If a child shows great potential, what can a coach or parent do to foster it? Should the child specialize or play other sports? Is early specialization in a sport good or bad? This chapter will introduce several key concepts: LTAD (Long Term Athletic Development), Stages of Development and Functional Literacy. These concepts will give you an understanding of the importance of movement for your junior golfer. Here you will find arguments that early movement is vital to success in later years.

> *"The central research finding is that no one becomes a world-class expert without ten years or more of intense attention to training and practice in the area of expertise. World-class experts may be defined as the top few hundred persons in any domain: Olympic winners in sports, concert pianists who win international prizes, strong chess Grandmasters, Nobel Prize winners in science, and members of national academies, and the like." (Bloom, 1985; Hayes, 1988)*

Herbert Simon won the Nobel Prize in Economics (1978) partly for his research into the role of knowledge in expertise. Mr. Simon coined the phrase: "Overnight Success starts ten years earlier." It was his research that led to many experts in the scientific field to agree on the aspect of a player reaching elite levels of performance after ten years of training.

Subsequent research has debated the familiar "10,000-hour rule" that says it generally takes 10,000 hours of dedicated practice to be able to achieve world-class status in any endeavor. Regardless, the predictions of this research are clear: becoming highly proficient at any endeavor requires training. There is probably not a parent on the face of the earth who does not wish for their children to be elite at something.

If you are wondering if your child is a prodigy, let's take a look at some true prodigies. Bobby Fisher won the United States Chess Championship at fourteen. He became a Grandmaster during the World Chess Championships qualification cycle at fifteen. Wayne Gretzky was skating with ten-year-olds at the age of six. At age ten, he scored 378 goals and had 139 assists in just eighty-five games! At the age of six, Willie Mosconi played against professional pool players. Prodigal children cannot be hidden. They will demonstrate their abilities on a national and international level quickly.

For sake of discussion, I have created the following classification categories. Where do you think your child fits?

- Highly Talented. Children in this group have accomplishments that do not merit the distinction of a prodigy. Nonetheless, they are competing at a much higher level than other children.

- Average. Children in this group are developing in growth, maturation, and physical literacy at the same rate as most children. Obviously, this is, by far, the largest group of children.

- Below Average. Children in this group have not developed their physical literacy, have not matured or have not developed at a traditional rate. Note that if parents keep a perfectly normal child from joining the world of physical literacy, movement and rules to help them mature, children can easily fall into this group.

- Challenged. Children in this group may have a life-altering physical or mental condition.

I have found that, generally, parents bump their children up one class level. The talented one becomes the prodigy. The average one becomes the talented one. The below average nine-year-old child is viewed as average. We, as parents, often do not look deeply enough into our children and make an honest assessment of their prowess in a certain area. It is hard to do. After all, they do go from crawling at two years to riding a bike at five. By age six or so, they are competing in many areas of mental and physical literacy.

Chances are your child is average, unless you brought them up in an environment where physical and mental literacy has been taught intensely. If that is the case, they may be talented or even demonstrate some prodigal characteristics. How can you be sure that this "ability" continues? How can you be certain this "ability" grows?

"Imagine a man and a woman. Imagine a child and a family with its

concentric rings of youthful dreams and mature wisdom. Does a picture come to mind? I'll bet one does, and I'd say it's probably a motion picture." Pete Egoscue, in <u>The Egoscue Method of Health Through Motion.</u>

To continue the ability your child exhibits, keep them moving. On the path to stardom are many footsteps. They must learn as many fundamental sports and movement skills as possible. Movement is the basic building block of sport and life. Sitting around worrying about how your child is going to fix their backswing should be a low priority. Placing your child in a competitive arena with the goal of winning should also be a low priority. The fundamental reason for children to compete is to have them move. Heck, simply playing more with other children is movement— often unstructured playing is joyous movement.

People of all ages must move enough to keep their bodies healthy. For a child, they must run, jump, throw and kick in all directions. Early specialization, such as only swinging a golf club, will almost always cause dysfunction in the muscular/ skeletal system. The athlete will work around this dysfunction until they are injured or until they simply hate the sport. What children need is bilateral function. They need movement in every plane of motion.

Emphasis on Multiple Types of Movement

The emphasis should be put on: awareness (kinesthetic), throwing, kicking, dribbling (and all manner of object manipulation), balance, coordination, speed, changing directions, running, jumping, dodging, skipping, hopping, bounding, and sprinting. Building physical fitness through movement is the reason children should play sports at an early age. Children today simply do not get a daily dose of movement. IPads and the Internet have replaced a walk to the library, making their physical literacy generally low.

Suppose you and your child walk into our Teaching Center. You believe golf is a sport where anyone can become proficient. Your child is ten. You are driven, aren't you? You want what is best for your child. You want them to feel the pride that comes with accomplishment. I am not yet emotionally attached to your child. I want them to uncover their physical and mental literacy. We are going to do so through golf. Can you imagine what goes on in my mind when I see a child swing a golf club with no sense of the impending strike of the ball?

I coached a player to win the US Kids World Championship at age nine. Another one of my students won the Mississippi State Amateur at age sixteen—the youngest champion in the history of the competition. Are they prodigies? Are they talented? The truth is they both have a high level of competency with fundamental movement skills. In these two examples, their ability to strike, throw and kick, for example, is so good that breaking through the "proficiency barrier" of winning a golf tournament is highly likely. Without their competency in fundamental movements, I doubt whether either of them would ever win such a golf tournament.

We all look at our children and ask, "Who are you?" Sometimes we ask this in a negative sense and sometimes in a positive sense. When you are motivated by a compulsion to help your children, I urge you to select **movement** first. Stay away from the definitions of talented or average or below average. It is evident to me that children that move in multiple planes of motion versus children who do not move will be deemed more talented.

We are driven to perform for a desired outcome. The problem is we seldom look into the process of the outcome. The process of fundamental movement skills or physical literacy should be the **first place** you go to help your child with any sport. You do not have to worry about what sport they should play. Instead, worry about the daily dose of movement your children receive. Remember, if you want to change the outcome, you must change the process. As in the Biblical parable, you must add fertilizer to the soil if you expect the tree to bear fruit.

Sports such as table tennis, dart throwing, Frisbee and racquetball train the wrists both in speed and accuracy. Wrist release patterns are basically subconscious or automatic responses. Playing these sports will definitely enhance chipping, pitching and clubface control.

Baseball, football, basketball, discus and javelin train children to generate power and accuracy. Soccer, martial arts, boxing or volleyball teach striking. Proficiency at striking a golf ball, for example, combines the ability to create force from the ground (i.e., throwing) and the ability to deliver a strike (i.e., boxing).

Golf is a sport of both power and geometry. Tennis and baseball are other sports in which players strike an object with an implement. Traditionally, tennis players catch onto golf more quickly than baseball players for two reasons. First, the striking weight shift in tennis is like the striking weight shift in golf. Note that the striking weight shift in baseball differs from the weight shifts in tennis and golf. Also, a tennis racket has a face, like a golf club, so the player can affect the ball flight.

> *"Kids who have fun playing a sport are more likely to stay active and healthy for their entire lifetime. They also have a better chance of becoming a top athlete. So, make it fun, and make it quality."* Canadian Sport Centres

Growth Velocities

Even though your child might not have an obvious physical challenge, there is an important lesson here. Have you noticed children growing at different rates? Peak Growth Velocity is the maximum rate of growth that occurs during the pubertal growth spurt. During a child's development there will be growth velocities and these velocities can offer windows of opportunity for children to learn or give them fits. When the children's bodies begin to grow, their growth generally means they will be dysfunctional. Their body cannot function according to its natural as bones, muscles, tendons and ligaments do not grow at the same time. Children will adjust to these differences on a sub-conscious level.

These growth velocities often make it difficult to assess talent. Early development, or early growth velocities, generally leads to a lack of coordination. As a child gets acclimated to growing bones and changing muscles, they are often overshadowed by late-developing children. Consequently, a parent or coach mistakes a lack of coordination or speed with early developmental growth. Sometimes early development leads to a labeling of "she is your basketball player," or "he is your golfer." Development, whether early or late, has its pros and cons. The early developer will have a physical advantage in the short run. The late developer has a better chance of creating a great work ethic in the long run.

I call another factor that hinders talent assessment, "societal complexity." Physical literacy can be defined as the development of movement skills and sport skills. Children who are raised in a society of movement will gain physical literacy. Children raised in a society of knowledge will gain communication literacy—they will gain reading and writing skills.

The task of defining talent is difficult. Is the child talented? Or, are their growth, maturation and society better suited for whatever it is we call "talent?"

Another, more subtle, hindrance to assessing talent is different types of sports. There are early specialization sports such as gymnastics and figure skating. Early specialized sports can be defined as a sport in which the player will be retiring at fourteen to sixteen years of age. If your child wants to win an Olympic gold medal, early specialization in gymnastics is critical. Beginning to flip around at age seventeen just will not do the trick.

There are late specialization sports such as football and golf. These can be defined as a sport where full potential is not met until after full growth maturity. When entering these different types of sporting events, the "definition" of talent, prodigy or average will obviously change.

The young stars of today, like Venus and Serena Williams or Tiger Woods, have led many parents to believe their child should also specialize early. Perhaps this conclusion is valid. But the vast majority of children will not have the physiological or psychological function to merit early specialization.

Dysfunction

In this context, I define "dysfunction" as the inability of the body to function according to its design. I define "compensation" as what the body substitutes when dysfunction is present. Depending on your child's goal, they could be physically inhibited because of necessary compensations created in response to various dysfunctions. The quickest way for a child to become dysfunctional is to be consistently dormant. That is, they do not exhibit movement in any plane of motion and continue to fail to exhibit movement.

When our children move, it is not simple movement that causes pain or injuries. Pain or injuries occur because muscles that were never intended to be used for a particular motion are called in to make up for the dysfunctional muscles. The muscle and skeletal systems are designed for movement. As children go through various growth velocities, they may have a little trouble "talking to these muscles." In effect, we are all inhibited, or at least dysfunctional, as we grow. All children will go through cycles of dysfunction.

All of us are prone to injury through lack of movement. We can all feel dysfunctions, or at least compensations, every morning as we celebrate our fortieth or fiftieth birthday. You might know someone in these age classes who complain of aching shoulders, hips or lower backs.

Istvan Balyi developed the long-term athletic development model in 1990 and points out there is a "variability to trainability." A child will pick up on movement at different rates depending on competence in functional movement, where they are in their growth velocity and the drill or exercise they are doing. In this way, placing a child in a box labeled talented, average- or below average becomes even more incorrect. It is likely what we deem talented is simply being asymptomatic functionally, having a foundation of movement (parents), and having unknowingly been cross-training with movement. Talent could simply be function in a world of dysfunction!

At one time I was deemed to be a talented boxer. After getting in a fight on the school bus when I was nine years old, my father took me to the local boxing club. The coach could not believe how quickly I got the foot work and the movement around the ring. My punching style needed some help, but he told my father I was a "natural." You and I can probably imagine the pride my father felt. Behind the scenes, however, I was a very avid soccer and tennis player. Footwork and ball handling skills were a part of my life already, so moving around a ring to keep from getting hit came pretty easily to me. I was stamped as "talented" and in the beginning that really helped. I won fights, believed in myself and my self-image grew. At the national level it was a bit different, as evidenced by my curved nose. Was it that I was really less talented than the best boxers or was it something else?

LTAD Stages

You probably have similar stories. You go from a beginner to really good in a short time. It is as if there is no time table for you. You were talented! A Natural! Maybe your children are doing the same thing. Before we label them, let's look at an LTAD's stages of development. Have your children had the opportunity to gain functional literacy as they grew?

- **An Active Start** is the first stage. It is from birth to age six that children are highly involved in daily active play. Running around, jumping over walls, and tripping over the bicycle are keys to professional sports for a three-year-old. The fundamental movement skills and physical literacy skills are bred here. Movement milestones such as balancing on one foot, hopping on one foot, catching a bounced ball and heel to toe walking are important.

- **FUNdamentals** is the second phase. This phase is from age six to eight for girls and age six to nine for boys. Here, agility, balance, coordination and speed are learned. The focus is on fun when learning the fundamentals of movement skills. A variety of sports and physical activities should be stressed and formal competition minimized.

- **Learning to Train** is the "Golden Age of Learning." Fundamental sport skills are built from their fundamental movement skills. Children are ready for formalized methods with a number of activities, girls are eight to eleven-years-old, and the boys are nine to twelve-years-old. It will be tempting to specialize in a specific sport or even a particular position in a sport. Premature specialization, however, will not promote bilateral movement and will increase the likelihood of injury.

- **Train to Train** is for the eleven to fifteen-year-year-old female and the twelve to sixteen-year-old male. This stage will "make or break" the athlete. Some will show special talents and true interest in the sport. Nonetheless, there should still be considerable time spent on training skills and general physical fitness. Time should be divided into half for training and half for competition.

- **Train to Compete** is for the fifteen to twenty-one-year-old female and the sixteen to twenty-three-year-old male. This is the "serious" stage of athletic development. These athletes are committed and are generally known as "aspiring" athletes. These children have recognized their talent and are generally committed to one sport. Here we find high levels of competition, nutrition, sport performance training and exercise.

- **Train to Win** is the final stage of performance. There are big trophies to be had and the athletes are now pursuing their sport full time. They train to maintain and maximize their performance. For girls, this begins at age eighteen and for boys it's nineteen.

- **Active for Life** is the final stage. Maybe Train to Train didn't work out as planned. Still, athletes have a great base for activity for the rest of their lives.

As parents, what do we do when our children are in the eleven to fifteen age bracket and many of us are on an active hunt for a sport for our children to play? The children in this age group, however, do not have a great physical base built. They need to engage in something seriously, so we take them to the best coaches and push them to become competitive. We are just praying they will "get it" so they can get a college scholarship or, at least, have something to showcase their talents.

Let's read the quote at the beginning of the chapter once again:

> *"The central research finding is that no one becomes a world-class expert without ten years or more of intense attention to training and practice in the area of expertise. World-class experts may be defined as the top few hundred person in any domain: Olympic winners in sports, concert pianists who win international prizes, strong chess Grandmasters, Nobel Prize winners in science, and members of national academies, and the*

like." (Bloom, 1985; Hayes, 1988)

Whether it is exactly 10,000 hours or ten years of intense training, it will take an enormous amount of work to be world class at any endeavor. For children, I believe it also takes a great base of fundamental movement skills and fundamental multi-sport skills. Movement will help our children build their athleticism with function—not working around dysfunction.

Golf is a PGA Professional's passion. They strive to give children the best opportunities to become as good as they wish to be. Consequently, when a youngster stands in front of me and starts talking about ball flight or what their right hand is doing, I am not really listening. I am watching them move. I am learning about their fundamental movement skills. I am learning about their past experiences as a human. I am figuring out how their parents were driven and how they drove them.

A sense of reason and logic must come to mind here. From birth to age six, before air conditioning, cable channels and video games, kids were moving. Agility, balance, coordination and speed were learned as kids road bikes, jumped over ditches and walked across fallen trees. At about age nine, most children or parents were not worried about travel teams or college sports. Pick up games of baseball, soccer, football and golf were created by the children. After all, why come inside the house? There was nothing to do! At about age eleven, mom and dad could not take them everywhere, so children began to carve their own paths in sports. By age sixteen or seventeen, everyone knew how good they were.

Times are different now. College football (one of my favorite sports) is more like a theatrical act than the game "Rudy" played. People return in droves to their alma mater to re-vist old memories or to share new ones. The parents and the kids look at the excitement around them. The kid is in....all in. He wants to play here! Now mom and dad have been busy, and the child is already nine years old. Video games and the Disney channel are more the norm than riding a bike seven miles a day. This is a sticky situation.

Often times PGA Professionals are on the other end of this "stickiness." The child and the parents are now ready for competition. It is time to pave their road to college. Often times, I remind them that climbing the ladder from learning to play to learning to compete takes time.

The point here is that we simply ***must get out of the habit of placing children in the box of talented or average or below average.*** Physical literacy is learned just like reading or writing or arithmetic. You and I must be driven to excel at the process of helping our children grow their physical literacy. The ***process is primary.***

The first step in the process is to get children moving. The process does not begin by teaching your child to keep their head down when hitting a driver or expecting a win in the junior golf tournament. At age seven, eight, or even ten, the process is all about movement. That is, which team your child plays on, or if they make the "select" team, trophies are not important to the process. Movement forms the base of the process.

If you find yourself being angry or frustrated because your son or daughter is losing golf tournaments at age ten, then you are not involved in the process. I am sorry to tell you that. There is nothing wrong with you. Before you get too deeply invested into pushing your son or daughter into full-time instruction (or ten tournaments each year), look into their movement.

If you find that your children have not followed the "perfect" model of fundamental movement skills, then join the club. Very few people have. So do not waste your time over what has passed. Karate, boxing, tennis and soccer are great sports that cross train golf. If your young child has not participated in these cross training sports, do not despair. Another big growth velocity, where your children will have a really great chance of picking up all types of motion through training, occurs around puberty.

Entertain ideas of the process and functional movement literacy. Entertain the idea of multiple sports that are not necessarily for competition. So what if the coach keeps moving my seven year old from goalie to forward? So what if the coach keeps moving your son from first base to the outfield? So what if my son gets outrun or outkicked? So what? They are learning, just like the rest of us. Keep them busy with movement and the dividends will be great. Just make sure the movement is in all directions.

In terms of golf, the worst idea for your child is to go to a driving range and hit golf balls for two hours a day. It does not matter if they are being coached or instructed for the entire two hours. I don't care. Simple ball pounding is a terrible idea. Get the children instruction, sure, but get them on the course. Let them play. Don't worry so much about their swings. Tell them to hit the golf ball hard at a young age. Keep their clubs short and do not let them get bored on the course.

If your child is older, in puberty, keep them playing multiple sports. You might fear they will be injured in other sports. But keep in mind that keeping them out of other sports has a dramatic negative effect on the sport in which they might specialize. Here in the South, we think there are two sports: football and spring football. Your child does not have to play football to increase their range of motion. Activities like karate or Parisi Speed School or some other "non-specific" sport helps your child move in multiple planes.

Yoga, Egoscue, and Pilates might not be favorite activities for your sons and daughters. They are, however, great for getting the body moving in different planes. Bilateral disfunctions are bound to happen when the body moves in a limited number of directions. Postural Analysis or TPI screens are useful because the human body is a bilateral machine. It should be monitored so it can remain at its functional peak, wherever that might be. Think of it like this. *Who would possibly think that eliminating mobility from a child's workout is a brilliant idea?*

I have taught two children who specialized much too quickly. Sadly, it was my fault. Both went to small private schools, and historically these schools have produced athletes who could not compete at the Division I level. I pushed them to specialize at golf—with mixed results. One student burned out by sixteen, but eventually came back to the game and is now playing at a Division II school. The other was offered golf scholarships, but not at the school he wanted. He went on to be a leader in student government and will soon receive his undergraduate degree.

I am sharing this story with you is because it is easy to remove, or reduce, movement and insert, or increase, specialization. Fundamental movement skills form the base for specialzation. I believe children should not specialize in a sport until they are sixteen years old or older. That doesn't mean they can't love a certain sport—it just means they must move in multiple planes. Invest in your children through movement. The dividends for them will be great.

Let me explain why I focus on movement. There are three planes of motion: Sagittal, Frontal and Transverse. Golf is a very rotary, so the shape of the swing is very dependent on how well someone rotates. If the athlete has not ever turned before; golf is going to be hard. If the athlete can't distinguish between "turning" and "tilting," we will be working on this PHYSICAL aspect of movement. Identifying the compensation in the swing is easy, but asking an athlete to move in a way they have never moved in is not.

The purpose of multiple sports and activities is for movement. If you or I believe the best players in the world are built technically, our thinking is false. Elite players touch on five key areas: Equipment, Physical, Technical, Strategical, and Neurological.

Chapter Lessons:

- It is going to take many years of intense training to reach elite levels of performance.

- Understand the competency level of your children in fundamental movements, but do not put them in a box of "talented" or "average."

- The body requires movement for health.

- Play multiple sports to cross train your children.

- Do not focus on winning when your children are young—focus on movement.

- There are seven developemental stages. To become good takes time.

- They are your children, so keep them moving in as many directions as possible.

ONLY ONE SHOT

3

1ˢᵗ *JTG*

James T. Gallagher was hired to help the greens superintendent at Meshingomesia Country Club in May of 1961. Originally from Pennsylvania, he and his wife Janie and children Jim Jr., Jeff and Jackie moved to the Marion, Indiana, club via a want ad in *Golfdom Magazine*. Jim would eventually become the club's PGA Professional.

Their first son, Jim Gallagher Jr., as the world of golf would know him, was only two months old when they moved to Indiana. By 1993, Jimmy was a rookie at the 30th Ryder Cup Match at the Belfry in Warwickshire, England, and by 1995 had five PGA Tour wins. Long before this, if one were looking for little Jimmy Gallagher, they would need to visit a small home between the 6th tee and the 9th tee in Marion.

Jimmy Gallagher Jr. won and for a bit of time he won a lot. He was celebrated and his achievements are still discussed in certain circles. The real richness of a champion does not come from the trophies though; it comes from hours and hours of honing their game and how that effort changes the person and their perception. The wealth of their stories can lead future generations of parents and aspiring professionals in the correct directions. Achievements last for only moments, understanding what lead to those achievements can last future generations a lifetime.

The house that Senior and Janie moved into in 1964 is still called home by the Gallagher family. James remembers Jim swinging at golf balls when he was only three years old.

"He would take empty soup cans, bury them in the front yard and play little holes that were maybe ten to thirty-five yards long. All the players at the club had to pass by in their carts and would get the biggest kick out of it. Some of them would stop and watch Jimmy and they would all have something to say to him, little words of encouragement like 'Knock it in little Jim.'

"Back then the country clubs were geared for the adults so there were a lot of restrictions on youngsters playing. So, Jimmy got a lot of his practice time in right there in the yard, chipping and putting on the rough terrain."

That adult-focused course was a lasting mindset from the 1950s until the 1990s for most clubs. There are reasonable explanations for this mindset, one of the biggest being the role of married couples at the time. Husbands went to country clubs, maybe for business or just to relax, and wives stayed home with the kids.

Another reason was the food culture. During the growth of the U.S. from 1900 to 1950 (as well as the advent of the automobile) a lot of roads were built. All of these new drivers needed dining options on their road trips. During the 1960s the "franchise" area of the US economy really began to boom. At first it was hamburger and pizza joints. Eventually franchises offered varieties of food and began to spring up all over the country. Before this boom of franchises, local country clubs were where families went out for dinner.

Combining the two components along with other cultural values of that time, it is easy to see why clubs were not focused on junior golfers. Today's world presents a different environment as women make up a larger portion of the professional workforce.

This has brought about a shift in modern country clubs. They are more dedicated to junior golf and are more family-focused. This idea has changed the pricing of club dues and has also changed the responsibilities of PGA professionals. In the past, mom, dad or maybe a friend taught youngsters the game. Today that role is more likely filled by a golf club's pro.

Senior was a pro from the "Old School." "Jimmy and his mom would go out in the evenings when the course was virtually empty," Senior remembered. "He would get to play a couple of holes, but for the most part he honed his game right there around the house."

As I listened to Senior recount this story, three factors came to mind. First is the simple fact of being bored. Without video games and cable television, there was little to do inside so getting outside had more appeal. The second factor was proximity. In 2015, I went to New York to do a few things for Golf Magazine. As one would expect, junior golf is not huge in New York City as there are attractions such as world-class museums, parks and historical landmarks. In Jimmy's case, outside his doors were golfers and a golf course. Taking nothing away from Jimmy and the energy he put into his game, we must recognize the importance of proximity and the possible distractions that technology can bring to children.

The **third** component is documented from Charles Duhigg's research on habits. Habits work in a simple structure: Cue – Routine – Reward. It is simple to find the external cues for a young Jimmy; each day he witnessed golfers and his father going to work at the course. Somewhere in the middle of this activity Jimmy, as a three- year-old, picked up on the cue and began the routine of trying to hit the golf ball in those tin cans buried in his front yard. The key here is the reward. The reward in this setting for Jimmy was the admiration and cheering he received from the practice. When he looked over his shoulder and saw his father smiling as members "hooted and hollered" at his accomplishments, it drove the habit deeper and deeper. Before long the habit of going into the front yard and hitting those balls around was habitualized. Duhigg's research of habits that led to his cycle of: Cue – Routine – Reward was probably seen more as a "gift" by those watching it. In reality it was a "gift" of circumstances.

This type of cycle of boredom, combined with a devoted family, proximity, and habit is very powerful. For yourself or for someone you are trying to help find their "gift," I would offer this advice: get close to it a lot and stay with it.

Jim Senior reflects on Jimmy's habits, "By the age of seven or eight Jim could go out and play each evening once the course was nearly empty. He had to play a lot of golf by himself because his age group hadn't taken the game up yet and the older ones didn't want a little kid tagging along. Today when I hear youngsters say, 'I don't take up golf because my friends don't play.' You don't need anybody to play golf with. You have a golf course and a challenge out there.

"Jimmy nearly always could get on the golf course late in the evenings and play nine or eighteen holes each day. He always had a tournament with himself and it was his Titleist 1 ball versus his Titleist 2 ball."

"How did you do Jimmy?" Senior would ask.

"Well Dad, Titleist 1 beat Titleist 2 by three shots," Jimmy would say.

"Anyway, the score changed and sometimes the other ball won but he would have a little tournament with two balls every time he played. He always had competition and played against the course. I reminded him so often that golf was a challenge between him and the course and I know he got tired of hearing it."

Senior was making golf a challenge for Jimmy and teaching him in a good way. Renowned psychologists Elizabeth and Robert Bjork have studied this process and refer to it as **desirable difficulties**. The Bjorks have managed experiments and studied two broad categories that tie learning and performance together. They have identified that **a lot learning can take place without an increase in performance.** They have also i**dentified that significant learning does not always mark an increase in performance.** The Bjorks refer to "desirable" difficulties as difficulties that **"trigger encoding and retrieval processes that support learning, comprehension, and remembering."**

Senior was giving Jimmy two balls to hit. That is important. Things may have been much different if he told Jimmy to only play one ball and he must shoot even par. That would have pushed the difficulty into an area that could be defined as "undesirable." Senior was also giving Jimmy the challenge of "Titleist 1 versus Titleist 2." So, on each hole, or on each nine holes, Jimmy had a new challenge. It didn't have much to do with pars, birdies or bogeys but it had a lot to do with Jimmy learning from one ball to the next.

Notice where young Jimmy is honing his skills. He is not on a driving range hitting ball after ball. The Bjorks and other psychologists who study learning and performance have different terms for the different types of practice. **Block** practice is practicing the same thing over and over again. **Random** practice is mixing it up. **Interleaving** is practice of different tasks. An example of Block practice would be hitting sixty shots with a 7 iron. An example of Random practice would be hitting sixty shots with six different clubs; here the clubs would be switched after each shot. Interleaving practice would be hitting a driver, then a chip, then a putt, then a bunker shot, and so on.

Jimmy was using the golf course to practice the process of **interleaving,** which has been proven to strengthen the learning process. A unique quality that manygreat golfers share is the instinct of knowing how they can impact how well they perform or score. With young juniors the best example of this process of practicing on driving ranges versus the golf course can be seen everywhere in the world. While the young man on the driving range may hit thousands of 7 irons, he may learn to start the ball left or right, but he will not be learning how that affects his scoring. A young boy or girl who is playing hundreds of rounds of golf will learn how a 7 iron that is pushed will affect their score.

"When he became a teenager, I sometimes had a hard time with him when it came to practice on the range." Senior continues. "I would tell him, 'Jim you know you are going to have to work on your swing too. You are going to have to hit some balls and see what the ball flight is doing. You are going to have to hit some different practice shots.' Jimmy would always come back and tell me how he liked to practice on the course. He would talk about hitting the shots on the course, with a yardage in mind and that he believed that helped him more. In the back of my mind I knew that all that playing would lead to this, but I had a decision to make. Does he learn the game first and then learn to practice or does he learn to practice and then learn the game? I chose the former and still to this day he is not much of a 'practicer.'

"He was such a feel player, even as a kid, that my wife and I had to team up to supervise his fundamentals. Jimmy just didn't understand mechanics as well as he did feel. So early on my wife and I would work together. We would discuss his grip or his ball position or whatever it was that was getting a little off. She was good at it. She could spot it when Jimmy was getting a little off and help him when I wasn't around."

It is easy to see that Jimmy's young golf life was void of driving ranges, the latest in technology and even other kids to play the game with. Looking at this out of context, it may seem like something anyone could do. Looking closer you see the importance of **proximity to golf, willing parents or mentors and challenges that foster learning by creating desirable difficulties**. As Senior talks about Jimmy's ability to get "out of trouble" I want to make another point. In the world of coaching golf, we often refer to this as **recovery shots**. The rule is simple: **get out of trouble in ONE SHOT!** The psychology of being in trouble is a bit different. Often when I take a player into the edges of the fairway with overhanging limbs and other hazards, the player reflects on how bad the shot must have been to get there. The very best players in the world routinely hit the ball into bunkers, trees and rough. The decisions made in those situations are pivotal. When a golfer never practices these shots, they will rarely be able to make the appropriate decision.

"One of the tools that helped him become a world-class player was his ability to be a trouble shooter. When he was playing at a higher level, I would see him hit some rescue shots that were unbelievable. I would ask him how he did it. 'Dad, I practice those type of shots. I put balls down under a tree and see which way I can curve it to get it on the green.' Jim did it more by trial and error than having the coach stand over his shoulders and tell him how to do it. It was really something to watch when he was at his best. He just teed that ball up on the first hole and played like a mad man to beat everybody. He didn't care if it landed in the tall stuff or the short stuff. I think a lot of that goes back to growing up and playing a lot of golf. "

The base line for skill development is movement. Because of this I was very interested to see if Senior had given Jimmy movements to practice around the house. Think of this as a stepping ground. First, we should be able to do something slowly without a ball, next quickly without a ball and so on until finally we are doing it with a ball.

"In the evenings around the house I think I would drop some seeds of knowledge. When he started to play every day, we were always talking about the swing or showing him how to execute it around the dinner table. I didn't have the time to be out watching him all of the time at that young age. Now when he became an older and more serious player, we would have a "session" scheduled. We called it a "session" instead of a lesson. By then, I took the time, even if I didn't have it.

"Jim was playing competitive golf when he was maybe ten years old. At the age of fourteen he shot 68, 71, and 72 and won the Grant County Tournament. The course played around 6,000 yards. The greens were pretty hairy in those days with only single row irrigation."

A normal ten or eleven-year-old shooting 68, 71, or 72 from 6,000 yards, which would be equivalent to the senior tees at most clubs, is astounding for an outsider to peer in and see. The human body and mind are nothing short of amazing and it is a little dumbfounding how a four-year-old whacking at the ground can have that type of ability on a golf course ten years later.

Rather than "prodigious gifts," Jimmy's successes were built upon proximity to the sport and his parents' knowledge. He had very little to do other than play golf and played with and without supervision. His skills were honed on the course of play, not on a driving range. He built skills among the constant variables that a golfer would face. This type of activity done consistently over a four-year period would increase the performance of nearly any athlete at any age!

This insight underscores the first major point of the chapter. Deal makers in business become very good at putting deals together because of their **proximity** to watching and learning to make deals happen. Authors become authors because of their **proximity** to books and writing. Basketball players would not be basketball players without **proximity** to a basketball court. To be great at anything, it takes **proximity** at a minimum.

Proximity matters and it may be the most important part of becoming who you are. John Tillery, a coach on the PGA Tour, resides in Madison, Georgia. JT has grown as a budding young coach with wins on every major tour and took Kevin Kisner from an unknown Web.com player to a multiple-time PGA Tour champion. JT is really good at something else too...he is really good at understanding people.

JT has the ability to understand a person, literally within minutes and what they are acclimated too, and what they expect to hear. If you were to listen to him teaching and coaching all day you would hear a huge change in his discussions as he relates to the person in front of him and the way he delivers his coaching methods. It is truly awesome to watch, and the basis of his genius is that he understands the individual standing in front of him has learned with different **proximities to different types of coaching and life culture** than the next guy has. As for JT, he grew up with a bell curve of different influences in his life, from golfers to lead musicians in famous rock bands. Even in the world of coaching, the proximity to influences rings true.

Proximity is a fundamental to talent development. It is not always simply how close you are to the game. It is how close you are to either your game or the 'person of interests game.' You can live on the golf course, but not play. You can get your kids training from the best teachers in the world but not take them to the course and you are burning your money. You can take lessons from the best teachers on earth and not practice what they prescribe, and you are still burning your money.

Don't confuse proximity with sitting on the sidelines. A grandparent may come to watch their grandchild play golf and simply enjoy the views, while the parent watching the same child play golf may see the phenomenal putting and great execution of their routine. Both are there, but they are perceiving different things. **Proximity** means getting in the middle of it.

It really doesn't matter if you are a golfer looking to get better, a parent looking to grow the spirit of the sport you love or somewhere in between, when your emotions begin to stir about accomplishing what is in your heart, don't get lost. The very first item of concern should be proximity.

Teen Years

When Jimmy entered his teen years, we made more of an effort to try and take him different places." Senior recalls. "He was traveling to statewide tournaments by the age of fourteen. The amazing thing was he never won the state junior. There was a guy, Larry Gosewehr and he was Jim's needle in the side. If Jim shot 71, Larry would shoot 70.

"Jim went down to the Orange Bowl International Tournament in Miami, Florida, when he was seventeen. He said Larry goofed off at the Orange Bowl but still beat him. I would always tell Jim to take care of himself and work hard. I always told him that par was a good score on any hole. I preached and preached to 'compete with the golf course.' If the hole was really tough don't try to birdie it. You can't control what other players are doing so don't spend your time thinking about them.

"The one problem that always stayed with him was slow players. He was always a good fast player and playing with slow groups always affected him. Some of that came from being the son of the golf pro and being taught to stay out of the members' way."

I have come to see the importance of travel and taking the game on the road over the years. It is not wise to stay at home, playing the same course time-after- time and then to expect to take it on the road and play your best golf. Larry was the first source of grit for Jimmy. Rivals are a deeply entrenched part of becoming a great player. Look back at the history of Ben Hogan and Bobby Jones and you will see early rivalries. Look at Nicklaus and Palmer. Every player who has ever played this game and every player who will play this game will encounter another tough competitor that pushes them.

With Larry we find the young man that is "gifted" and doesn't have to do much in preparation to shoot lower scores. Generally, this is found with early physical development, giving the junior golfer an extra thirty or forty yards off the tee. Many of today's young standouts in golf can chew up 70% of a golf course's total length with the driver alone. The math is pretty simple, given equal short games, strategy and emotional abilities. The kid hitting it thirty yards farther off the tee has quite an edge. While golf is a game of numbers, there is an internal scorecard that is harder to read that coexists with a player as they develop.

Grit. Grit can be defined as "an individual's passion for a particular long-term goal or end state, coupled with a powerful motivation to achieve their respective objective." (*Wikipedia*) Without Larry, Jimmy would not have needed Senior to remind him to stick to his own process and to take care of his own game. Jimmy never would have learned to **grow his grit** while a junior golfer. When a player gets to college and if they are fortunate enough to play on a major tour, they will find plenty of "Larrys" out there. It is very fortunate when each one of us has someone to push us and make us question our goals and our ability to achieve them. As Thomas Carlyle said, "No pressure; No diamonds."

There will be this moment in each golfer's development when they understand the real question is character development. It is a moment when they come to understand they are not "the best" on the course. As the age of competitive golf grows younger and younger, it is likely the parent will feel this as well. There will be a moment, generally lived over three days and fifteen hours at the golf course, when the parent realizes their junior golfer is not "the best" on the golf course. The character, grit, intelligence and love of the parent and child will be tested.

This generally happens when the athlete goes to college. The old timers called it moving to a "Big Pond" from a "Small Pond." Many freshmen or sophomore collegiate players went through the moment in their lives where they had to acknowledge that they must get better to achieve their goals or even make the team. Instead of having one "Larry" there were actually dozens. But away from the home, the college athlete also had additional daily responsibilities: to prepare or get meals, do laundry, attend class and prepare for a test in a setting where a professor may or may not know their name. It is a time of growing up and understanding there is more to this "life of mine than just a score."

Howard Gardner, a psychologist by trade, was the first to challenge the old beliefs of what it meant to be "smart." Gardner, and others now, believes our culture has placed too much emphasis on logical thinking and verbal abilities to determine what a "smart" person really is. Larry was obviously very "smart" when it came to striking a golf ball at a young age, apparently "smarter" than Jimmy was. But what of this grit? Much of this grit begins to arise when we learn that we are not as "smart" or as "good" as we thought we once were.

Gardner's research gives us seven intelligences. 1) Linguistic Intelligence, the Intelligence of words. 2) Logical Intelligence, the intelligence of numbers and logic. 3) Spatial Intelligence, thinking in pictures or images. 4) Musical Intelligence, the ability to perceive and create rhythms and melodies. 5) Bodily-Kinesthetic Intelligence, the intelligence of the physical self. 6) Interpersonal Intelligence, the ability to understand and work with other people. 7)

Intrapersonal Intelligence, the intelligence of the inner self. The majority of athletes are generally going to have a high intelligence quotient with their bodies, be proficient in interpersonal intelligence and have intelligence of their inner self.

Taking your game on the road as a youngster is important. Taking your game on the road as a grown person is important. Traveling early, Jimmy had to use and cultivate more of his intelligences on the road. He was forced to use spatial intelligence to understand the new courses. He was forced to use his interpersonal intelligence because he was traveling, generally with his mom. At home, Jimmy could just go play using his kinesthetic intelligence.

Jimmy underscores the importance of these intelligences as he tells his story. "It is important to learn to travel and compete. There are just so many things that have to be learned. Everyone who watches PGA Tour players is in awe of how they hit it or how they handle the pressure. That stuff really isn't that hard when you have control of your golf ball. The stuff that is hard is off the course. When you aren't hitting it good and need to clean some stuff up but don't feel like working on it. When you are at a big event and there are five or so holes that you just can't seem to fit in your mind's eye. I could give you hundreds of examples but there is more to playing great golf than just hitting the shots and making the putts."

A parent or coach can find a foothold that will really help the athlete climb to toward their goals. Traveling to play tournament with a mindset of learning (both the parent and the child) will develop other intelligences and grow the grit. The proximity to tournament golf is a gift that only a parent can give. The mind set of learning the course, learning from the win, learning from the loss, learning from the failure and growing from it is also a gift the parent of a young junior golfer controls.

For a tournament player, Visual and Intrapersonal Intelligences can't be taught or learned early enough. In golf we talk about being self-smart and seeing the shot. These two intelligences are boiled into one and called a "routine." You will hear this all the time around players so understand it is very simple; **it is a player performing the same physical cues before striking each shot.**

"I told him he had to have a routine," Senior begins. "Before you hit your shot you need to have pretty much the same routine. Get your yardage, select your club and target and then hit that shot with that club. Don't second-guess yourself. 'Whether it is the right one or the wrong one, it is the right one' I would often say. I encouraged him to picture the shot. After a while he could visualize the shot and could make the club move the ball around a bit. I did spend time with him on routine. I always stressed to him that he had to have a good view on where he was going, then address the ball and point the face at the target and go from there."

"I was always a quick player," Jimmy explains. "I also always took the same number of looks at the target once I was over the ball. I always walked in to hit the shot with the club in my right hand. It really didn't matter if I was twenty under par or even par, I would find my target, picture the shot, walk in with the club in my right hand, take one look, get settled, then take another look and hit it."

Routines have a rhythm, involved visualization, and involve physical acts. Routines involve trust and commitment and involve multiple intelligences. A tournament player learns to use these intelligences to produce efficient mental and emotional energy

"With regards to strategy, we talked about pins being placed behind bunkers but, instead…if you get it on the green you will be able to putt it," Senior recalls. "If you go for those corner pins you will sometimes not have a birdie putt and so on. **I taught him to be sensible and not to try and hit the**

greatest shot of your life every single shot. I heard something like that from Arnold Palmer years ago and thought it was a tremendous statement."

Routine and **Strategy** are important intelligences to grow. There are so many reasons for this type of training, and I know for certain there is only one place to truly apply them. It is easy for junior golfers to spend too much time on the driving range thinking of their body's movement while they swing the club. This is only one phase of training and not a very good one for getting the game to transfer to the golf course. This is also cultivation of Kinesthetic or Body intelligence, which is part of it, but only part of it.

Many, many times I hear parents or college coaches speak of an individual who "can't get out of their own way" because they are so mechanical. When a player becomes "too technical" are they self-sabotaging or simply going back to the intelligence they have grown? I would suggest that all athletes are adaptable, and science has taught us that our brains are very adaptable, so I would suggest that over-use of one intelligence can lead to a lack of growth in another intelligence. In the end, it is about being balanced. Senior was obviously cultivating this in a young Jimmy Gallagher.

There is also another intelligence, or something like an intelligence, that must be recognized: the notion of freedom. We all know people who get away from the nest and act in manners that no one would expect. The advertising slogan, "What Happens in Vegas, Stays in Vegas" is a great example.

There have been those who fall victim and are thrown off track by the Three Fumes: Alcohol, Gasoline and Fragrance (cologne or perfume). Typically, the fumes play out in this way. A youngster reaches legal driving age and gasoline is used to fuel their car. The car, just as the driver's license, is generally the first taste of freedom. This freedom usually leads to teenagers getting together and hanging out. Generally, this is where another "fume" will be found, fragrance. Being that neither the boys nor the girls are acclimated to this newfound freedom and proximity to one another, it is not long before the third and final "fume," alcohol, comes flying in.

A recent conversation with a Division 1 Golf Coach sums it up best. Walking around the golf course together at a junior golf event, I asked the question, "Are you seriously recruiting these thirteen, fourteen, and fifteen-year-olds when you are watching them play?" He responds, "It depends. Generally, at this age we want to see how they perform on the course. We want to get a good idea of their emotional stability and their mechanics. We want to get a good idea of their ball control and temperament. The more intense recruiting comes during their tenth- grade year generally."

The evidence of a young teen venturing through the Three Fumes is all around us. We have seen it time and time again. A talented young man or woman, derailed by the temptations that come with freedom, is nothing new. We have also seen this play out with world-class professionals in multiple sports. And yes, we have seen it play out in our own communities, with some thirty, forty and fifty-year-olds acting as if they were sixteen all over again.

"Jim's first car at sixteen was a used car that was big enough if so that if he had an accident he wouldn't be hurt," Senior began. "We never had any trouble with him not wanting to play. A lot of parents talked about their son or daughters spending less time playing golf when they started driving. With Jimmy the car as a symbol of freedom didn't pull him off the golf course at all. In fact, pretty soon after getting his ride he won the Grant County Championship at -19 under par. (The closest to him to this day is -12 under par.) Jim was around seventeen then and that record will hold for a very, very long time."

As Jim entered his teen years, he had proximity to a golf course, proximity to a great coach, and had developed some grit. He was also growing his intelligences or, as we call it, his golf IQ. The stage was set, and it was set pretty early.

The story of a young Jimmy Gallagher and some of the great players we see now on the PGA Tour is clearer through the ideology that there is more to winning than a golf swing and great chipping and putting. Long before anyone is watching or clapping there are parents and a community of people providing access to the golf club community and to instruction as well as access to learning situations that grow the intelligences.

Often overlooked is the idea that if intelligence must be learned, it cannot be taught. Enrolling your children or yourself in golf lessons will no doubt increase intelligence when it comes to swinging a golf club, but the student must be ready to put in the work. Often times in our society today we pay for education but may not put in enough time on our own to learn what we are paying for. Understand that a golf lesson is just the beginning. It is up to the individual to put in quality reps and learn. Coaching and supervision are worth the effort because the athlete can be assured the reps are being done correctly.

The same holds true on the golf course. Each shot requires the intelligence of math, visualization, self and rhythm to be brought to the table. Everyone should get on the golf course expecting to learn little pieces that collectively will make him or her a better player. Remaining on the range until you can hit the perfect tee shot is great, but you will need to know how to visually fit that shot into each hole and the rhythm you move in to re-create it time after time. There is no better place to become "self-smart" or improve your intrapersonal intelligence than the golf course.

"Jimmy rolled into his teen years pretty quickly," Senior begins. "While I was working and Janie was with three kids at home it seemed some of the days passed really slow for us at the time. Looking back on them now it happened in a flash," chuckled Senior. "We were all in with Jimmy, just like we were with our other two. If they worked hard at whatever they chose to do we were behind them 100%. That was our rule to one another as parents. We would give them chances and opportunities.

"Jimmy played in the Insurance Youth Classic at Napa Valley, California, at the age of sixteen, qualified for the USGA Junior in Colorado that year and played in The International Orange Bowl. I didn't hold him back from competition. In fact, if he wanted to play, we would do it. In 1982 he really started to blossom as a player. He won the State Am in 1982 and 1983 and won the Indiana State Open in 1983, his junior year at the University of Tennessee.

An apparent reality of accomplishment is often hidden in the shadows. It is the reality that we only have a certain amount of energy and time. For the Gallagher family it was obvious they had a clear end-goal for Jimmy, and nearly all their energy was aimed at the future of their children and Jimmy was in the crosshairs because he was their firstborn. Behind the "bright" future of Jimmy Gallagher Jr. sat two parents that were ready and willing to carry their children through the shadowy expanses of accomplishment. The family's threshold for failure, the family's expectations for the time and monetary investment are often not brought to the surface.

Senior re-counts chuckling. "Of course, there were tough times between Janie and me and the kids when it came to performance and preparation in life, much less the golf course. One of the things we just couldn't accept was a bad attitude, beating clubs on the ground or saying things like 'I suck' from our kids was not acceptable. Janie probably had to monitor that more than I did, but I know we were sticklers on those little things.

"Winning, accomplishment and preparing are all very far apart in nature," continues Senior. "Winning and accomplishment are fun. Winning big things and accomplishing big things are really fun. But preparing for those wins and achievements aren't always fun. It wasn't all that much fun for Janie to hop on an airplane with Jimmy and fly across the country while leaving me and the kids here on those trips. It wasn't much fun for me to work fourteen hours and then get meals prepared without Janie. But being a parent isn't about having fun all the time if your children are trying to win and accomplish goals. It is about being a parent and nurturing those goals and dreams of your children."

The truth is that accomplishment takes time. Failure is a part of the process. Maybe God gives this type of understanding to parents and participants. Maybe it can be learned. Just know that behind everyone you see on Sunday afternoon there are many behind the scenes that helped carry, and sometimes push, the individual through the slippery slopes of accomplishment.

Teen Years Practicing

"During the high school years, we made minor refinements to his swing. Jim had upright clubs and I always wanted the shaft of the club between his right shoulder and right ear. He was probably a much more upright swinger when he played his best. There was always a slight drop to the inside on the way down. When he was a teenager, he really didn't like mechanics. When we would go work on something like ball position and takeaway and he would say, 'Now wait a minute Dad. I can't work on two things at once.'

"Jimmy was like most good players. Early on they are eager to learn and eager to practice. As they get better and better, the ones that will be great are still eager to learn. The really great ones continue to want to learn even when everyone around them is telling them how great they are. Jimmy always wanted to learn. He really did. He would get a little mad if I gave him too many things to think about. I don't blame him for that.

"Jim had a lot of talent. He always had a sense of what it would take for him to put the club on the ball well. He had tendencies to slide a bit and others accused him of having a little bit of a reverse pivot because he stayed on his left side a little too long. But we didn't have to re-invent the wheel during his late teens. I always felt that building an efficient motion started at address. I did all I could to keep the ball forward in his stance, standing tall, with a good grip as he was growing up. I must have said something to Jimmy a thousand times about his set and grip over the years. He never wavered in listening and I think that is why he had a good motion as a teenager.

"Other golfers I have taught said things like 'I feel too close to it,' or 'This grip doesn't feel right,' but I never really listened to them. If I could see what the fundamental would do for their swing and efficiency I didn't mind if it was a little 'uncomfortable.' When they came back for the next lesson and the posture or grip had gone back to their old way, they were telling me more than they knew they were telling me. They weren't just saying I didn't like the change, they were saying they didn't like to learn. So, Jimmy and I had a lot of conversations about those types of things over the years.

"There is a lot to learning the game of golf," Senior continues. "It is not all just swing and how far the ball flies. There is the short game most people discount. **In all the years I taught I never saw a single chipping green that had more players on it than driving range.** That tells us something about golfers, they like to see the ball fly and get control of that thing in the air. But controlling the ball on the ground is very important.

"For a budding teen or a recreational golfer, being able to hit a bump and run or a pitch shot that finishes close to the hole will do more for their game than hitting fifty or so 7 irons. Jimmy and I talked a lot about being a balanced player, or at least practicing in a way that is balanced. Jimmy did a pretty good job through the years. I am talking adolescent and teen years of course.

Senior is breaking it down really simply: train your body when you can focus on it. Practice skills one at a time so you can focus on each one. Play the game with what you have trained and what you have practiced. In a sense Training would be the color **Black**. Playing would be the color **White**. Practice is the **Grey** area where internal skills are being used to produce an external skill.

Training and Playing are different. Training that is taken into practice has too much emphasis being placed on it, so the skill of getting the club or ball do a specific task is not working out because the player cannot accomplish the task. Then they internally turn to the "feels" of the training in an effort to accomplish the task of practice. The result is a negative one.

Training should have an internal focus that puts the athlete and the club at certain positions at certain times. Most of this type of "training" is done without a ball, or at a minimum done without concern where the ball is going.

Playing has an external focus that puts the athlete in efficient places in time to get the ball as close to the target as possible. The difference is where the focus is placed during the athletic motion. Is the focus external or internal? Answer that question and you will know if a player is "playing" or "training."

The **grey** area is where practice generally takes place. All over the world, at this very moment, players are losing time and getting frustrated because of this area of practice. The athlete is hitting a ball, with some desire to see the ball being efficiently struck. That desire may be in the realm of contact or direction, and the athletes themselves may only define that desire of efficiency. Where is the focus? If the focus is internal, then certainly the player is training and where the ball goes is not important. If the focus is external, then certainly the player is playing, and how they are swinging is not so important.

John Tillery, a tour coach that we spoke of earlier, has two very different and very gifted clients, Scott Brown and Kevin Kisner. During one of his coaching sessions with "Brownie" it became apparent when Scott was focusing on getting the club in a better position, the ball flight was not as efficient as when Brownie just

"Damn it, Brownie, I am asking you not to worry about the ball flight," JT said in a way that a southerner could understand.

"Yeah, I know you said that bud, but don't forget I am a tour player. That leaderboard over there doesn't have any swings on it, only numbers. When you ask me to put the club here and I hit one, I am gonna end up on the bottom of that board," Brownie said.

With that he pulled out a ball, put the club in the best position at the top of the swing the world of golf has ever seen, and hit a pull. "Now then, if I just go in there and think about hitting the back of that thing, my backswing is crap but now I am heading up that board," Brownie continued. With that he laced a five iron that never moved.

"Kiz....Kiz....you got a second?" JT asked. "Sure bud, what is up? You and Brownie talking golf swing again?" Kevin asked.

"Yes," JT replied.

"Well Brownie, all I can tell you is when JT and I are working, I pretend there is a net in front of me. If JT says do this or that, I concentrate on doing this or that. I don't really care where the ball goes because if my boy JT says my motion is getting more efficient, that is all I care about," Kevin said looking at both of them.

So, you get it huh? Two very successful athletes with the same coach, standing on the same range, with two different mindsets on where the focus should be. Here is another one that Mike Adams, one of the greatest coaches the game of golf has ever known, shared with me.

"I was on the range working with players at Doral in 1999 or 2000. I wrapped up my work with a few players and walked over to one of my friends, Butch Harmon, to say hello. Butch was standing behind Tiger, watching his ball flight. I walk up and say, 'Hello pro' and Butch and I made small talk for just a minute.

"Tiger ripped this long iron. Just crushed it. The ball never left his target and he turned to Butch and asked, 'Was that it?' Butch shook his head 'no.' Next ball Tiger catches a little thin. He turns again to Butch, 'How about that?' Butch shook his head 'no' again. The third ball Tiger hits behind and it flies out there like a wounded quail. He turns to Butch, 'How about that?' Butch nodded his head in agreement. 'That was it Tiger. That was the motion we are looking for,' Butch said.

"Tiger and Butch did amazing work together. Tiger trusted Butch and wanted to learn from him. I was really in awe of both of them after that little session that I observed. It taught me a lot about a player's ability to trust his coach, even if they were the biggest thing in the game," Mike said.

Players need to understand their WHY as well. Why are you practicing? Why do you want to get better at the game? In a nutshell, WHAT is your WHY? If what a player is after is a perfect swing, then simply answer WHY. If what a player is after is a college scholarship, then simply answer WHY. Communication is so key in this entire process. Communicating with yourself may be even the most important component of the key to communication.

WHY is why so important? The reason is because it will change. Your WHY for coaching, playing, competing, practicing and training will change. If your WHY changes and you don't realize it, inevitably problems arise in your game. It is the reason we say so often, "Emotion builds motion." If the WHY stays the same, typically the game will stay the same. When the WHY begins to shift, then the game begins to shift.

Jimmy never really liked mechanics. He loved playing. He loved accomplishing tasks in practice. He loved competition. But when it came to training or swing "stuff" Jimmy was never a fan and never really opened up to training.

Jimmy's dislike of mechanics is still prevalent today. Elite players will generally always want to accomplish something with a golf ball. After all, that internal drive to do something with a golf ball is partly the reason they are so good at the game. However, they must have a basis for the swing and mental pictures that are correct for the use of the club through the strike. If they don't have some basis in training, when it goes "south" it can really go "south." Most of the time the player will display this emotionally.

"Jim and I would have 'sessions' on the practice range." Senior recalls. "The simple reason was because of time. I was a workaholic. I would work seventy to eighty hours each week. So, we didn't get on the course that much to work on his game. Instead we would have 'sessions' on the range. When he became a pro, I would sneak off for a week but then get back and work seven days a week and work two shifts.

"Most of my tutoring was on the range. I would also caddy for him as much as I could. I tutored him around ball flight. He liked to work a little fade and Jim was long. When he played his best golf, his ball was falling a little left to right. He had a fairly neutral grip and his hands always seemed to set on the club well. I liked the Vardon grip but Jimmy chose the interlock grip. I always emphasized that the toe of the club should be pointing to the sky on the way back and then the toe pointing to the sky on the way through.

"We worked a lot on address, the distance he was from the ball and a lot on alignment and small changes to foot placement. I always told him to let the arms hang and let the bigger muscles get the club back. Once he started playing good golf we worked on just basics."

Senior left most of technical work to discussions around the house. Listening to his words, he demonstrated his ability as a world-class coach. With exception of "set-up" or addressing the ball properly, he was always talking to Jimmy about the club or ball flight. Research suggests a strong correlation between being comfortable with an athlete's focus being on external stimulus and high performance. High performing athletes are comfortable focusing on getting the ball to the target. Senior, while a self-described "workaholic" was a PGA Club Professional and over the year he figured out where a person's focus needed to be to perform well.

"I never witnessed his swing just get terrible. Even when he was away from me. Mike Malarkey, the coach at Tennessee, was a PGA Professional and I trusted him because of that. Jim was such a good player in Knoxville and for the team. He shot 61 at Cherokee in Knoxville and shot some low rounds. The biggest problem I had with Jim was speed of play. I would tell him to make sure he was READY TO HIT THAT SHOT and I didn't like slow play either. He learned to play that quickly as a kid because the golf course back then had a lot of play. That pace of play stayed with him his entire career. Jim became a better player by playing and playing and playing. From time to time I would check to make sure he was doing the right thing. I still think he was better being too fast than some guy that meditates over it.

With Jim that slow play would interfere with his thoughts and his game. So when he got paired with slow players, sometimes he couldn't handle it.

"Jim was a pretty typical about showing his emotions after a bad shot. Janie and I spoke with him about poor language after the shot. But Jimmy didn't take the bad shot with him. He was able to shred that shot off his shoulders and not carry it with him. He was never a 'club-thrower.' When he was a youngster, I would simply not allow poor behavior. When my kids were younger if they weren't happy with their game, I would put them to work. So if they didn't enjoy themselves on the course, I would give them something un-enjoyable to do off the golf course."

There is maybe no more controversial idea in the game of golf than the importance of winning. In football, the championship team can lose possibly one game per season at the most. In basketball, the championship team can lose possibly a dozen or more games. In contrast, golf at the highest level has seen only moments of players winning more than 40% of the time. Only the grand legends of the game (Jones, Nelson, Player, Palmer, Hogan, Nicklaus, Woods) have even come close to winning one third of the time during their very best years.

As a junior golfer this is different. Depending on the level, many junior golfers may win almost every event they play. Others may play at a very high level and have a list of great finishes but go years without a win. The controversy comes from the statistics of the past. In golf, winning just doesn't happen as often as most all other sports. So should winning be emphasized?

"I tried to instill in him to play and compete to the best of his ability. I told him he could only control his game and that if he was prepared and ready and did his best, he might not win but he should still go out to win. You have to feel like you are going to do your best win the tournament. Trying to win is important. When Jim was in a slump, I always tried to instill upon him to treat playing poorly like a learning experience. Let every tournament and every round of golf be a learning experience.

"We took Jimmy to different events knowing that he had a great chance to win and others where he would learn something from the older, better players. It was always better for him to play with someone better because he had to play his best golf. At home, Jim would primarily play with members when he was fifteen and older. I still remember when he first beat me. I shot 37 on nine holes and he shot 36. He was probably a freshman in high school.

"At school as a freshman he was the best player on the team but I asked the coach not to play him in the number one spot. They would put him in as the number two man and Jim just couldn't understand it. I would make up an excuse for the coach and tell Jim just to keep trying and he would get that number one spot. I didn't want him to get the big head. I didn't want him to walk around with his nose up in the air. I always wanted him to remember that his life would be a lot better if he got along with people rather than being a showoff. I tried to have him get along with people. I also did it so it would push him to play better."

Winning early and winning a lot can change players and their tolerance for failure. I personally spend a moderate amount of time with players and their families preparing a schedule. I will never forget Mike Taylor, winner of ten Mississippi State Amateur Championships, explain to me his ideas on preparing for a tournament. His plan was simple; he would give himself three tournaments before the "one" he wanted to win.

Growing evidence also suggests that it is important to win at every level. Whether this is because of the skill sets needed or the self-image created does not really matter here. What does matter is that competitive golfers build schedules with tournaments they can win, tournaments they might win and tournaments they have very little chance of winning.

It is easy to see Senior understood this concept and implemented it with Jimmy. From the tournament scheduling to the "little trick" he played on

Jimmy with the high school team. While most parents would be doing the very opposite, fighting for their child to play the position they earned, Senior went the other way. Almost as if to say, "Well Jimmy, the world isn't always fair. You take care of what you can take care of."

"One thing Jim did was become a lot better player by practicing on the golf course. He would drop balls in difficult situations and learn to hit those shots. Later, on tour, being a good trouble player was very good for him. I can remember him hitting some shots from trouble that were spectacular.

"Back then we didn't have 7 wedges. We had 56 degree wedges and he would hit as many good shots to short targets. The same with chipping and pitching around the green. Hit them the best you can and hit a bunch of them. When you find something you aren't good at, try another club. There wasn't a lot of bump and running up here for Jimmy. I grew up bumping and running it so I would have him feel like he was putting the ball with his 7 iron. On a lot of shots he would need to use the 56 degree. I liked the ball under the chin, with a little shaft lean, and to use steady eyes. I always felt like people didn't keep the eyes steady enough through the shot. I never had to fight with Jim to practice that. He would spend hours doing it. In fact, if I couldn't find him for a while, I could go to the short game area and find him.

"Same way with putting. Jim had a bunch of drills he would do that challenged him to make a certain amount. I can remember driving him back from a tournament and that very evening him wanting to go to the short game and practice. He picked a lot of drills himself on the putting green.

"I told him, "Remember Jim when we came to Indiana, I came on a $7.00 want add placed in _Golfdom Magazine_, and they told me that if I did a good enough job, I would keep it. I would tell him that he had the opportunity of a lifetime with the golf course right out the front door. What if you lived five miles from here and you couldn't get to the course? If he didn't become a good player after his dad helped him and his mom took him here and there to compete it would be his own fault. Kids that get their driver's license and don't go to the course are not going to be the champions, they are going to be 'also-rans.' So hard work and taking advantage of opportunities was something I lived and he was reminded of."

In the present day, we might call Senior an "old timer" or a "hard nose." The truth is Senior did the exact thing that sports psychologists are saying today. Senior helped Jimmy make better decisions. He cultivated, along with his wife, an environment that didn't hold Jimmy's hand the entire way. The environment was full of lessons for life and preparation for the future while balancing the present.

This idea of preparation for the future and balancing the present is also a big one. In Jimmy's future this concept would come up again and again as he and his wife Cissye began their family. What is important to unravel are the ever-changing answers to an emphasis on winning, or where and how to practice, or how important it is to train.

Mike Adams, 2017 PGA National Teacher of the Year, said it best to me one day. "Hey Veeg, you know the answer to EVERY question a player asks his coach when the coach doesn't know the circumstances the player has been in to prompt the question?"

"What's the answer, pro?" I ask.

"It depends!" Mike says with a warm laugh. "Every answer, to every athlete is dependent on what is going on in their game. I will share a little story with you, Veeg. I was coaching this guy on the PGA Tour in the mid 1990s. He was on a tear, finishing inside the top twenty every week. He was making every putt and asked me to look at his stroke.

"He had over a twenty-footer and took it back, made a big counter clockwise loop at the top of the stroke, opened the face, paused for a second and then moved the putter back down toward the ball. The ball rolled end over end into the hole.

"'Hit me another one,' I asked him.

"With that he hit me a dozen more, with the same loop in the stroke, and they all went in the hole. After a bit I asked him. 'Looks like they are all going in, what did you want me to look at?'

"'Well everyone is saying I have a loop in my stroke. I am putting good but I just wanted you to look and tell me if you saw anything weird.' He returned.

"'A loop! Don't listen to those guys. You are putting great and they are just messing with you. Keep seeing that ball go in the hole and doing what you are doing!' I told him.

"Veeg, the point is in that circumstance it didn't matter if the putter was looping or not. Later in the year, when he couldn't manage that stroke and began to miss putts, we took care of it. Given the circumstance the correct answer was for me to instill confidence in him and give him the permission to keep making putts, not to tell him his stroke was terrible. Later, after his run on the tour was coming to a close that year, he and I had a different conversation and the answer was different."

This early collection of Jim's years may not be where you are as a player, a parent or a coach. Many of the answers you will have, or do have, or did have can be answered in the above paragraphs. The guidelines used by Senior are very relevant today and will continue to be. Just remember the timing of the answers is really important and the secret is being open enough to truly understand that in the end, it does depend on the circumstance.

Create a safe and loving environment for yourself and others. As Jimmy grew from a junior golfer and headed into college, he knew his family believed in him and would give him all the opportunities to master the passion God had given him. All the times in planes, trains and automobiles had proved that. Words, as well as actions, prove this as well.

If there is a junior golfer in your life or if you are an amateur it would benefit you to listen and learn from the main themes here. Practicing on the course, playing more than hitting balls, staying external with your thoughts and putting an emphasis on preparation are just a few. Specifically, for the parents of a junior, look at the sacrifices. Also, many parents say they want the best for their children. Wanting the best for them is going to cost you something. More importantly, just because it costs you something doesn't mean your threshold of failure should change.

Ask yourself and those around you to answer their WHY with the understanding they may not be playing the game for the same reason. Golf is a great game for many reasons. You don't have to play it for other people's reasons; just know your WHY and let that be enough for now.

4

UNDERWATER BB STACKING

Practice. What is it? Why do some people build great golf motions, but most cannot? Why do most golfers only experience frustration when they practice? This chapter introduces several key concepts: Deliberate Practice, The 70/30 Rule, Testing Versus Practicing, and Noisy Feedback. These concepts will serve you well as your junior golfer grows in the game and give you the ability to discuss the reasons behind spending hours at the golf course. That is, why are you at the golf course? Are you there to test your skills? Are you there to build a better motion? Are you spending too much time testing instead of practicing? It is important to have a frame of reference for being at the golf course.

Three Stages of Practice

- **Practice**, like nearly every movement, decision or motivation goes through three stages.

- **Anticipation.** Anticipation can happen when you are going to a baseball game, when meeting someone new or just heading home after work. We always anticipate that which we are aware of happening in the future.

- **Action.** So now we are in the middle of it. We are experiencing the ball game, looking the person in the eye or we are with our family at home.

- **Reinforcement.** The action is over. Did the ball game end the way we wanted? Did the family have a good evening? What problems were solved? What funny thing happened?

The power of these three stages makes practice so important and so difficult to understand. Everyone goes to the lesson tee anticipating something. During the action phase they are working on something. As they walk away from the practice area, they are re-enforcing something. The same stages occur on the golf course. The same stages happen during competition.

Disappointment during the action phase is generally the reason golfers come to our Teaching Center. My clients want only one thing—to become better golfers. They want their golf ball to fly more often in the direction they are intending. Many of my new clients believe I will say something to them or simply give them a feeling that will instantly fix their ball flight. This belief is simply incorrect. I have no magic words. I can't give someone a feeling. I can, however, tell them the exact area where they can change a feeling. The feeling that they build for themselves depends on how they practice.

No Thinking and Swinging

People are held back at this sport because they "think they can think" during their swing. Unfortunately, nothing is further from the truth. The brain, muscles and skeletal system have rules that govern how well they perform together. It is not just the brain or the muscles. It is the whole package—down to the ligaments and tendons and beyond. If you want to learn something right now, learn this: **Stop Teaching Yourself to Think about Your Swing While You Are Hitting a Golf Ball**

When I was a youngster, my dad, Vic Trolio, said something I will never forget: "VJ Trolio, you are going to be great at something, even if it is underwater bb stacking!" I have had thirty years to build a visual of "underwater bb stacking." I don't know where my dad came up with this statement, (he is famous for his off-the- cuff sayings) but it gives a great visual of what practice should be.

Practice should be tougher than competition. Practice should have a single focus. Practice should build on top of a base and that base is movement. Practice should be deliberate. Practice should reinforce proper movements. Practice should build proper movements.

"It's a miracle that the modern methods of instruction have not entirely strangled all curiosity of inquiry." ---Albert Einstein

The Place to Practice: Think Ben Hogan and Bobby Jones

One of the biggest problem areas in becoming better at golf is that people generally believe the place to practice is a driving range. The modern method of standing on a driving range and beating balls is critically flawed. Driving ranges are profit centers and fun places. They are easier than the golf course, they force you to focus on ball flight and the swing, and they disguise your flaws and lead to improper movements.

Mr. Ben Hogan was widely known for practicing. People still speak of the way Mr. Hogan "dug it out of the dirt," but many do not know the whole story. Mr. Hogan went broke twice before being successful at golf. He would become famous for his victories and his intentional practice sessions. Before becoming famous, he was just another golfer. Mr. Hogan did not become a champion by practicing at a driving range. He was infamous for practicing at what is called "The Little Nine" at his home club, Shady Oaks. I have been there. There are all types of elevation changes and slopes. Large oak trees line the Little Nine on both sides—which easily simulate a hole. There are multiple targets. Bottom line: The Little Nine is definitely NOT a driving range.

A look into Mr. Hogan's early years and practice sheds light on his ideas of how to get better at golf. First, understand that Mr. Hogan had "Hennie Bogan" who had "an insatiable desire to practice and was a greater golfer even than the great Bobby Jones." Hennie was a make-believe character who told Mr. Hogan to practice. Moreover, Mr. Hogan did not have access to hundreds of golf balls, he only had what would fit in a shag bag. As a kid, Mr. Hogan jumped on the course with a group of kids and played. He got his start as a caddy, standing beside his "loop" and watching them swing.

How many children caddy these days? How many shag golf balls for themselves? How many are hitting toward a human (generally a caddy) standing in the middle of a field? How many are jumping on the course with a group of children and playing? Finally, how many have an imaginary player, better than even the great Bobby Jones, standing next to them judging their work and shot? Doesn't the word "deliberate" come to mind when you read this account of Mr. Hogan's practice?

Because Mr. Hogan held Mr. Bobby Jones in such high esteem, let's take a look at Bobby Jones. It seems someone cut down a "cleek" when Bobby was about five years old. Before this, as the story goes, Bobby was trying to wield a club which was much too big for him. After getting his "new" club, Bobby and his friend (both five-years-olds) laid out a golf course in the front yard. They played the golf course as a daily event. There was no instruction or advice other than: play the ball as it lies and all strikes count.

The Jones family moved to Atlanta because of young Bobby's medical condition. There he found Stewart Maiden, a Scottish player who was the resident professional of East Lake Golf Club. Young Bobby began following Stewart around the course, watching his every move. Before Bobby was seven, he was given permission to play except on Saturdays and Sundays. After school, when he couldn't play, he would practice on the thirteenth green which sat behind his house. He chipped the ball up and putted until the ball was holed. "Pitch to the green and then putt out, pitch to the green and putt out." Does the phrase "deliberate versus mindless" come to mind?

The Form of Practice in Today's World

Practice today is far different, isn't it? The parent drops the child off at the course. They probably meet a group of friends at the driving range. They hit shots, concerned more with who hits it farther and who can to hit the range picker. Soon bored, they go in and grab something to eat. Then, they are off to the pool or to the break room. They are not out watching the best players play. They spend much more time at the practice area than getting out on the course, constituting a day often deemed to be practice. After all, the child spent nearly three hours hitting shots, chipping and putting.

Let's look at golf instruction. Lessons come at an early age and are mostly given at the driving range. The kids are told, or it is implied, that the driving range is where one comes to practice. They are taught, usually through words, to do this or that with their swings. They are taught to think about their swings and judge ball flight. Albert Einstein was right! Most modern practice programs and facilities stifle the chance of learning.

> *"Self-education is the only real education that there is. Schools and instruction advice can only make self-education easier. Beyond that, they do little."* ---Isaac Asimov

Watching and Deliberate Practice

Bobby Jones and Ben Hogan watched. They watched players. They used their eyes to learn. Jones and Hogan played the game. They got on the course—or they built courses. Jones and Hogan worked deliberately on their game. Although they educated themselves, they did it deliberately. Whether it was the young Jones glaring at Stewart Maiden's swing or the young Hogan being coached by Hennie, it was deliberate.

Here is the definition of Deliberate Practice: "**Being engaged in activities specifically designed to improve performance with full concentration. It is daily practice done in a work-like manner with a specific goal of improving performance. Moreover, Deliberate Practice, requires high levels of effort and attention and is frequently not enjoyable.**"

Is it easier to dump out twenty balls and chip them, or to do as the young Bobby Jones did and pitch one ball and putt it out? Is it easier to stand on the range and hit fifty balls without a target or to have twenty balls that you must pick up yourself as Mr. Hogan did?

Getting better always comes back to the same thing: deliberation in practice. Great junior golfers are deliberate. They enter the practice session with the anticipation of accomplishing a single task. During the action phase of their deliberate practice, they accomplish this task. The re-enforcement comes from seeing the process and creating the outcome they desire. Great juniors do it every day—except on Sunday, of course. Our juniors practice mostly at home, away from the driving range. They do it where they can see themselves do it and for a defined amount of time. Instruction points them in a direction and the students self-educate.

My junior golfers who struggle do not practice each day. In fact, they practice more before a tournament—which is the opposite of what one should do. The focus of their sessions is not on a single task. The action phase gets lost because of poor shots, an undefined session or someone talking to them. The excuses never end. Because the action phase is not defined, their re-enforcement is not clear. They get lost in the many variables that can affect practice. In effect, they are not practicing— they are taking tests on how well they are controlling their ball. The only problem is that they have not studied for these tests.

Why is it that some junior golfers can stick to the process and some seemingly cannot? From my research, the difference stems from the ability or inability to control emotions during a practice session. It starts early, as you probably know. We all have memories of our children wailing, with tears pouring from their eyes, because they couldn't have a five-cent sucker. From the beginning it is very easy to get emotional when things aren't going our way. This same behavior, while maybe not as dramatic, can be seen all around the world from children on the driving range.

The Effects of Practicing Mindlessly

I will go out on a limb and suggest that parents to aspiring golfers can either help their children or hurt them when it comes to practice. By this, I mean a parent can either re-enforce their **child's practice habits** or the **outcome of the child's practice habits**. I am speaking of a session on a driving range, not a tournament. There are certainly times when the outcome of a process, such as a scoring slump or a constant bogey finish, must be looked at. The danger lies in when the parent becomes emotionally hijacked by the flight of the ball on the driving range. That teaches the child to act like a child.

Deliberate practice is simply different. It stands as a dividing line between taking control of the things you can control and accepting the things you cannot. Deliberate practice uses as many senses as possible. Deliberate practice minimizes variables and maximizes learning. Deliberate practice is defined. In a sense, deliberate practice gets rid of frustration while building motion.

As a youngster, I experienced the effects of practice that was not deliberate. The first time was after the USGA Junior. I made the cut but noticed a need for enhanced ball striking. At the time Nick Faldo was atop the world, so I took his book to the range and opened it up. There were lots of pictures and drills to follow and I worked hard for the majority of the fall and winter. By spring I was worse. It was not because Faldo was wrong; it was because I messed up in the anticipation phase.

I had no golf instructor. Further, I did not understand how boggled the anticipation phase was in my mind. At the time I was convinced that a swing could be found. Just a feeling and click, you are on your way. Every time I did one of the drills my concentration was more on the outcome of the shot (while I was doing the drill) than the movement itself. All my work took place at the driving range. There were no mirrors, no video and most importantly, no separation between the drill and ball flight.

To get out of my slump, I just went back to playing golf. I was a self-pronounced "player" that simply did not benefit from instruction or drills. I experienced these same series of events after my freshman year at Southern Miss. I had made every tournament as a freshman but, because the team was going to be young my second year, Coach Sam Hall redshirted me. Back to the range I went, this time with even more golf balls! As a youngster I had to shag balls myself. Now that I was in college, I had access to a fifty-five-gallon drum full of golf balls every day. Of course, history repeated itself. In reflection, I believe that was the worst period in my golf life— trying hard to get better but getting worse.

The Building Blocks of Deliberate Practice

Learning begins in the anticipation phase. Building a swing or a stroke simply takes time. Your son or daughter will not just "find it." They will build it deliberately one day at a time. They should anticipate the fact that they are getting one percent better each day. They should anticipate that their motion is changing day by day. They should also anticipate working on it each day for a certain amount of time.

There is no evidence to support the idea that hard work in the beginning allows your junior golfer to coast into the future. The game of golf is a tendency of sorts, and the body, as we now know, is ever changing. While some experts might put in deliberate practice of three to five hours daily, your child should not be pushed to do this. I always suggest five minutes a day, or possibly thirty repetitions a day, 300 days each year.

While performing deliberate practice, your children should learn to "Look, look and look!" One of my first mentors as a teacher was Ben Doyle, who resides in Carmel, California. Ben was always saying, "Look, look and look!" During the action phase of building a motion, your juniors need to use every sense they can. Obviously, taste, smell and sound (auditory feedback is awesome if you can find it) will not do them too much good. Day in and day out they are left with two senses: sight and feel. For children, more times than not, they will stop looking and embrace the feel without verifying where the club actually is during the drill. This is a bad habit and a bad idea.

A simple fact is that the more you do something, the harder it is to feel. As children's muscles, tendons, ligaments and skeleton move in a certain way, their feel will change. This development is normal. But you must keep your junior golfer looking. They must take the time to understand how the movement feels. Take the time necessary to relate the movement to something they have done before. Take the time to describe how the movement feels. During the action phase of deliberate practice, the only things that will not change are the drill and having the player look and feel. After all, golf swings, as with all programs of movement, are built at a cellular level. Therefore, the length and tension relationship between muscles will change through movement.

This aspect of deliberate practice is so important for the youngster to understand because this aspect is where they will build (or solidify) their motions for the rest of their lives. Most juniors stop improving because they never appreciate highly refined practice and the complexities that come with it. Deliberate practice is not rocket science, but you should do it daily and you must "Look, look and look!"

Proper Reinforcement

Let's turn our attention to reinforcement. When kids come in for a lesson, they just light up when they see how their swings have changed. It is hard for them to believe that all that swinging in front of the mirror has changed their motion so much. But look closely at what we are doing: we are placing the primary attention on their swings, not on ball flight. Some will say, "Hey! Paying attention to swinging is great. But all that matters is where the ball is going." I agree—if you are playing in a tournament. It is important to remember your child is wielding the club and inputting all the data into the ball. The ball responds to the delivery of the club. So, what is more important: the swing or the ball flight? Does the club react to the swing? Yes. Does the ball react to the club? Yes.

There is no doubt that the motion is more important than the resulting ball flight. What you must teach your children is to reinforce their process of deliberate practice rather than where the ball flies. When the golfer succeeds through the process of deliberate practice, the ball will start going where they want it to go. We must always reinforce the process. We must not reinforce the outcome. Giving way to sloppy practice habits and then scolding your child after a bad round is not sound thinking. I know that I am in the business of helping people with their outcome. But to help people with their outcome, I almost always have to fix their process.

The 70/30 Rule

The instructor, (i.e., me) only accounts for thirty percent of your child's success. I simply cannot reinforce everything your child learns from me. You, the parent, and the process you create, grow and emphasize accounts for the other seventy percent. Steering your child away from outcome and into the process is truly a team approach. The instructor needs to be a professional and give the correct information. The child needs to understand the motions and how often they should be done. The parent needs to reinforce the importance of the process during practice (and what practice really is). When we are learning new motions, we must not focus on the outcome.

If the process is correct, advancement becomes very simple. The child wants to get better. They are taken to an instructor. The instructor says do this drill 600 times and come back. The child goes home and the parent holds them accountable for doing it thirty times daily for twenty days. If the outcome is not better, then the instructor might need to be replaced. Pretty simple, wouldn't you say?

But let me throw a little wrench into this cycle. You must remember that it is the brain that learns the new pattern, not the muscle. Standing somewhere and repeating a motion mindlessly is not the same as practicing with intention.

Practicing with Intention

There are two basic ways to practice with intention, randomized practice and block practice. A deliberate golfer engages in **randomized practice** when he or she randomizes the task at hand. A deliberate golfer engages in **block practice** when attempting an exact task repeatedly. In study-after-study, you should know that **randomized intention** leads to greater retention than **block intention.**

A simple math example shows the difference between these two ways. Note that in both cases, the goal is to add two numbers together.

- This series of questions illustrates block practice: What is 213 + 33? What is 213 + 33? What is 213 + 33? What is 213 + 33? By the second time you read the question, you probably didn't have to think. You probably just answered the third question. By the fourth time you read the question, you might have been wondering, "What in the world am I reading?"

- This series of questions is an example of random practice: What is 234 + 14? What is 312 + 41? What is 563 + 11? This series of questions makes you think, doesn't it?

- Deliberate practice should make your child think by using random practice. You must look for intention as well as motion.

The reality is that your mind controls your muscles! To build a motion, the repetitions must be done through block practice. When a junior golfer does nothing more than repeat the same motion over and over, they will overstate their confidence level. Then when thrown into a game full of variables, (golf) they will fail. Therefore, on the driving range, the junior golfer must practice in a more random manner. That is, putting with one ball as they go through their normal putting routine. Or, when striking the ball, the junior changes clubs and targets from shot-to-shot while going through their normal full swing routine.

Watching some of the best players practice over the years has shown me that when players are really engaged (deliberate) in the drill, they will most likely randomize the motion. In other words, they will do the drill with a club, without a club and possibly with different clubs. Their bodies integrate the "feel" as their minds are thinking about hitting certain shots. An important lesson is that the mind is extremely engaged during deliberate practice.

There are important caveats for practice sessions. As boredom, fatigue or frustration set in, the performance will change? Boredom generally sets in because the session is lacking intention and deliberation. Fatigue generally sets in because the practice session is not defined. Frustration generally sets in because the feedback isn't provided effectively.

While boredom and fatigue are really self-explanatory, proper feedback is not. Feedback should **not** be done as frequent, immediate and informatively as possible. It is really a myth that we will perform better with constant, immediate feedback. Do not be the parent standing behind the child giving feedback constantly. Be patient on the range (or course) and let the child learn. Look for your chances to give feedback effectively.

If the practice process is incorrectly implemented, things become complicated. The child wants to get better. The instructor gives them a tip or two. The child goes to the range and the tip immediately feels uncomfortable. The ball flies sideways. The parent sees the shot and calls other folks to verify if the instructor is, in fact, a good one. After this investigation the parent concludes that the instructor is a good one. Without reinforcement from the parent, the child starts to go back to what is comfortable. The parent, emotionally attached to outcome, thinks that as long as the outcome is fine, everything else must be fine. Maybe the golf gods will somehow get that club in a better place at the top. Who knows? The child is happy. Golf, however, remains a mystery. Notice that there is no accountability on the instructor, the child or the parent. How can one expect improvement?

Here is an example of doing the practice process correctly. The child does the repetitions daily. When doing the repetitions, the child's mind is involved. The child is looking, using different clubs and using imagery while making the motion. The motion is doing two things: building the motor pattern and providing the "feel." At the course the child would be doing one of two things: building the pattern without concern of ball flight or testing the feel while going through their routines. The child takes the information from the tests and goes back to the deliberate practice for more acquisition of the skill. Notice that the outcome is ignored. In this example, improvement is highly likely.

But eventually outcome does matter. Let's see where by talking about testing and tests. Testing is performance based to see what the player has retained through deliberate practice. Therefore, testing cannot be called practice in any sense. Examples of tests are making ten, three-foot putts in a row, hitting a high draw and then a high fade, tournaments, or any number of other events where a player is "testing" their feel. As you can imagine, the number of tests is practically limitless. The main lesson is to understand that testing is not practice. Practice focuses on building feel and repeatable patterns. Testing measures how much of these focus areas are retained.

Deliberate Practice, Reinforcement and Confidence

Let's return our focus to deliberate practice. Here are some specific examples:

- In front of a mirror, practice the correct ball position with a ball and alignment sticks.

- Stand on a wobble board and make putting strokes.

- Stand in front of a mirror while adjusting the top of the swing to a more neutral position (while looking at the position, of course).

- Sit on the couch and work on the grip by putting the club in the hands properly, waggling it, and then do it again.

Deliberate practice comes in all shapes and forms. Deliberate practice is done for a set amount of time or repetitions and the player is actively trying to accomplish the task at hand.

Let us examine the role of reinforcement in the deliberate practice context. Suppose a player is trying to adjust his motion while being emotionally attached to the outcome of the shot. This attachment makes improvement difficult to accomplish for both the player and the instructor. Even for the best players and instructor duos, practicing while having outcome attachment is difficult. When standing behind a tour player, instructors can assess swing issues easily.

When we start heading down the road of building swing thoughts and feelings, we, as a team, must be extremely careful. The difference between tour players and your junior golfer is vast. Many tour players already have built their motion at a cellular level—with little compensation. The tour player has a subconscious skill set filled with talent. Your child is building his motion and skill set.

I once had a very interesting conversation with a multiple winner on the tour about a leading sport psychologist. The tour player commented that, early in his career, he focused a lot on physical cues in his routine—like looks and waggles. Over the years the sport psychologist figured out if the best players in the world commit to the shot each time, their routines were the same. So, for the player and his psychologist, there was a shift in focus. Physical cues became less important than getting "committed" to the upcoming shot.

This sport psychologist has written many books and helped thousands of golfers on every level. If you picked up one of his books now, you would see less emphasis on physical routines and more emphasis on getting involved in the target. When information is disseminated across a broad range of different skill levels, some information will be targeted to a small specific group and some information will be targeted to larger groups.

I think that every junior golfer could improve his sport with specific movements during the swing. I also think that junior golfers naturally have a hero or icon. They want to act, practice, walk and talk like these people. They want their golf ball to fly like the golf ball of their hero. The danger of this way of thinking is that junior golfers might put too much emphasis on ball flight. Consequently, practice becomes very sloppy. The same can happen if score is the focus. You, the parent, might think: "Tiger shot thirty-nine at age seven and so did Johnny today." This focus is dangerous. If one overlooks fundamental movement skills, sport specific skills and the intricacies of deliberate practice and focuses instead on the outcome of score, your junior golfer simply will not become all they could be in the game of golf.

Remember: you, the parent, are seventy percent of the equation. If you judge your child based on something they can control, like deliberate practice, you will greatly influence the rate at which your child builds confidence. Think of it like this: **confidence is skill acquisition.** With the emphasis of acquiring skills in an area your child can control (i.e., deliberate practice), confidence will come. Here is an example of building confidence using deliberate practice. Building connection (that is, upper arms against the chest) in the golf swing by practicing it twenty times nightly is completely in the hands of the child. The result will be that the child's swing is connected while hitting a seven iron over water to a tucked pin on a firm green. This accomplishment comes from a group of skills including connection and confidence. Both skills are a result of deliberate practice.

Deliberate Practice Focuses on One Skill at a Time

- Deliberate practice does not cluster skill acquisition. Deliberate practice focuses on a single skill. More examples:

- Work on the grip ten times.

- Work on the set up ten times.

- Work on getting into the lead leg ten times.

Importantly, separate these areas if you do them every day. Or just focus on one area every day. After a couple of weeks your child will find it easier and easier to do what they are practicing, and their confidence grows as they acquire the skill.

Clustering skill acquisition will defeat the child nearly every single time when they are first learning the game. What do I mean by clustering skill acquisition? Here is an example. Little Johnny stands on the range. After a couple of misses, an onlooker trying to be helpful might say: "Keep your head down." Little Johnny hits one good one, and then misses a few more. The onlooker adds: "You need to turn a little more." Immediately a bad shot occurs. The onlooker says: "No, no, not like that. Keep your knees flexed." A good shot results but it is followed by three more poor shots. The onlooker states: "Get your back to the target now at the top of your swing." What is going on? In this example there are four skills being clustered all the while the ball flight is being reviewed.

Here is an example of deliberate practice with a focus on one skill. The parent might say: "Let's do a little work today. I want you to make some practice swings with a balanced finish." The first swing is a little shaky. The second one is a little better. The next one is close. "Keep going, Johnny, until I see five good swings in a row. Then you can hit a shot." After fifteen or so attempts, Johnny gets five in a row nailed perfectly. The parent might add: "Hit a shot and hold the finish until the ball stops rolling." Little Johnny tops the ball, but he holds the finish until the ball stops rolling. The parent exudes: "Great job kiddo! Let's see five more perfect finishes!" What is going on here? One skill set with the child being rewarded. Note that the reward is not for the outcome (which he can't control), but for the motion (which is under his control).

It is obvious which example above will have little Johnny leaving the driving range with confidence. The sad part is many of you who represent the seventy percent of the equation, do not follow this type of deliberate practice and behavioral therapy. Instead, you often get involved in the ball flight, get emotionally sabotaged with the outcome and try to fix the outcome. Please be careful. Make certain that you are helping your child acquire skills. Make sure you are leading them through the action phase of practice properly. Make sure you are reinforcing something that they can control (motion). Strive not to reinforce something they cannot control (ball flight).

Deliberate Practice and Noise

In truth, golf is a game of variables. These variables are what make golf so difficult. The wind often changes during the round. The pin locations change daily. The putting surface changes throughout the day. For skill acquisition (aka confidence) to grow the instructor, the practice and the parent cannot be variables. Instead, they must focus on what is desired during a session of practice and must make certain what is desired is something the child can control. Clustering skills (variables) and judging ball flight (variable) while judging the shot as good or bad as a parent (variable) is a recipe for frustration.

Deliberate practice is more than just mirror work or drills—it is where your mind is, too! Here are some examples. Playing golf with your friends where score is not kept versus playing golf with your friends with a medal on the line. Your son stands on the range hitting at a target an unknown distance away versus hitting at a target ninety-eight yards away. Standing on the range hitting balls while you think your ball position is good versus hitting balls with sticks lying down giving you your ball position.

You see, deliberate practice is not what you are doing; it is how you are doing it. The simple reason is feedback. For your son or daughter to get better, they must get proper feedback. The scary thing, and possibly the most difficult concept, is trying to keep the "noise" out of the feedback. To me, noise is a way to describe the lack of learning that can take place during a practice session. Often, parents identify the enemy of their child's success as their child talking and laughing with their friends while hitting ball after ball on the range. I believe noise goes much deeper than this jocularity.

Noise can come from the mind, the body, the parent, the coach or any other variable when the intent of practice is not defined. As we saw earlier in this chapter, the parents who stand behind their child chiming off ten different thoughts are obviously noise. A body that is having trouble moving because of a growth spurt or dysfunction is noise. A coach that is constantly changing the message is noise. A mind that is not concentrated on the task at hand can create noise.

Deliberate Practice Has Inten

A cornerstone to practice, deliberate practice at least, is to have the intent to accomplish a specific task during the session. This intent might be to figure out, and then practice, hitting high bunker shots. The intent could be on learning to punch out from the trees with a six iron. The intent might be on a weight shift or a steady head. **There must be intent.** There must also be the awareness that the junior golfer easily loses intent. Strange as it may sound, practicing for three minutes with intent is far better than practicing for fifteen without intent.

Children can learn, unfortunately, to practice with noise all the time. They just hit the ball, hear a voice, make an assumption, change something and then hit another ball. This cycle can be repeated and repeated without any intent. Then, when they enter a tournament, the noise really turns on. Dad is watching. The scorecard is in the back pocket. Everyone will be looking at the scores. Kids are everywhere hitting all kinds of shots. Remember, if these children have not really worked on anything deliberately, their scores change dramatically for the worse during tournament play. **There is so much noise the children cannot get feedback on what their job is that day of practice or in that tournament.**

This lack of feedback or noise bleeds its way through the anticipation phase of practice. It appears in the action phase when the child is not being intent. It also forms a cloud over the reinforcement phase. "My child just doesn't have it," parents will say. "He just can't control his emotions on the course." Actually, your child is probably not being intent in his practice. Your child is most likely a bit confused by what they should actually be doing during practice. There is nothing wrong with your child—the process that he is practicing is wrong. Again, nothing is wrong with your child—it is the fact that they are practicing the wrong kind of "practice."

Clustering Tasks Creates a Lot of Noise

Deliberate practice eliminates as much noise as possible. Your child is deliberately practicing when they are regularly practicing with intent and focusing on one area that needs to be fixed. This area could be mental, physical or technical. I recommend that they not be mixed or clustered. In other words, if your child is working on his routine, do not worry about the swing. If your child is working on her technique, do not worry about where the ball flies. If your child is working on physical skill, leave the swing reminders out.

When a player is simultaneously working on ball flight, technique and routine there is simply too much noise. When a player is on the course working on their swing while judging their score, there is too much noise. This type of task clustering makes it nearly impossible to practice with intent. Sounds simple, doesn't it? I suspect clustering tasks is where parents make their most dreadful decisions and their biggest mistakes.

Parents must help their children focus on a single task. This task might be a specific type of bunker shot. Obviously, the club face must be open and the club path will be a bit outside to inside. First have your youngster set up with an open face and make swings outside to in. Then draw a line in the sand and have them make the same motion with the same face and hit the spot they are looking at. Note that a ball has not been hit yet. Ask them to do this drill twenty times each day. After they have made their twenty motions, bring the ball into the equation. If all is good, then hit some shots; as soon as difficulty begins, get rid of the ball. This is a great example of deliberate practice because the process has intent. The intent is to acquire and master the ability of swinging the club out to in with an open face and hitting the sand where the child wishes. Simply hitting bunker shots is not deliberate because intention is lost when the focus is on ball flight.

Your child should do this for two to three weeks for a certain amount of time each day during practice. Follow a schedule of practice. I assure you that PGA Tour players do not have to do this each practice session because they are already experts at it. Look closely at the practice sessions on Tour and you will see "mini sessions" of these intentional motions all the time. As your child progresses, you can create another deliberate practice session after three weeks or so. Maybe the focus will be on an even more open face or possibly the task is to work on the routine in the bunker. Whatever the case, always define the intention of the practice for your child. Remember: **at first, keep the ball out of the equation and put attention on the process.**

The Path to Excellence

I hope you are now thinking that the path to excellence requires hours of intentional effort. It does. Remember: **practice must be something that your child can control and must be intentional.** Dumping out a pile of range balls and hitting at a target is not practice. Taking your child to the range and expecting them to think about their golf swing while you judge their ball flight is not practice. These "practice" attempts are far too noisy! On the other hand, having your child practice a simple task such as ball position for ten minutes and then taking them on the course and having them intentionally run their mental routines is practice. **Confidence is skill acquisition** because a child can work on ball position and then they can run their routines on the course.

Nearly every week I give a lesson to someone who believes he can think his way through the golf swing. You probably experience the same type of people in everyday life, those that just keep adding and adding until you can almost hear the noise. **Becoming proficient, or elite, at a movement is really a result of electrical impulses carried through about 100 billion "wires" between our ears.** They are basically God's wiring, with neurons being connected together through synapses. The bunker shot, the chip shot or simply the grip are by-products of a fancy light show going on at a cellular level.

Muscle Memory really doesn't exist. Simply stated, the more we use a motion, the more the electrical impulses fires until the circuitry is built at a cellular level. This circuitry development at a cellular level is then seen or felt as being second nature, hence the concept of muscle memory. This area is a tricky one, because those players that have created "great circuitry" will often tell you they have always possessed the skill. It is a grand illusion. I have never seen a child hold a club for the first time and then swing it with competence.

Physiology and Deliberate Practice

> *"Have you ever stopped to think that movement is as much of a biological imperative as food and water? It is. There was a time, and not long ago, when it was easy, instinctive, to obey the biological imperative of motion."*
> ---Pete Egoscue

So, we grab a ball and toss it in the air. We toss it again. We toss it again. What is happening? The neurons and synapses fire (electrical impulses) to make the motion, other cellular bodies, oligodendrocytes, sense the commotion and gets in the middle of the party. These cells, the oligodendrocytes, then begin to wrap and squeeze on the electrical impulse finally leaving behind a sheath like structure called myelin. **Myelin is what transforms a movement from a "dial-up connection" to a "broadband connection."**

Deliberate practice fires the electrical impulses again, and again, and again. The whole time, at a cellular level, another event is taking place as the oligodendrocytes are getting in the mix. These cells are grasping, wrapping and spinning around the impulse thereby insulating and speeding it up. Skill acquisition happens at a cellular level. This is why skill acquisition takes time. The exact amount of time cannot be readily estimated because our brains seemingly get different amounts of myelin at different times.

Eventually the deliberate practice of throwing the ball into the air has created a cellular change. The electrical impulse from the neuron to the synapse has been encased in a sleek pathway, thanks to myelin. Finally throwing the ball into the air is quite simple or even second nature. As you can see, it is not the cognitive thought that creates this skill; it is the reaction of movement at a cellular level.

This cellular activity reacts to movement. You cannot think your way to this cellular reaction. You cannot think your way to elite movement. The firing of the circuitry must take place time and time and time again. It requires action. It requires a mind. Building cellular reaction is why movement in multiple planes is so important. Building cellular reaction is why practicing intently or deliberately is so important. Because cellular change takes place over time, the establishment of a designed practice regiment is the pathway to acquiring cellular reaction.

It is also apparent that age matters. It appears that myelin is more prominent in stages or waves. The variables are not completely known but two of them are DNA and activity. An early start, or at least a timely start, can be crucial. As we all know, being at the right place at the right time can make all the difference. It appears this same concept applies on a cellular level as well. Getting the right movements, in the right context, at the right times is very important.

Research supports the idea that elite performance happens at a cellular level. It is not a child winning and then gaining the confidence to continue to win that creates a great golfer. On the contrary, is the firing of the neurons and the deliberate practice that gives the child a winning movement pattern.

A Short Final Thought

Please do not get the cart before the horse. Do not seek a win to applaud. Instead, insist on steady, deliberate practice and let the chips fall where they may. Applaud the practice and understand the process is slow, steady and difficult. Failure, after all, is the backbone of success. The road to mediocrity is smooth. The road to elite performance is strenuous, long and as rough as the surface of the moon.

Practice can be playing golf and working on your routine. Practice can be learning to read different lies around the green. Practice can be in front of a mirror doing a drill. Playing four holes and really concentrating on a particular task each day is much better than playing fifty-four holes on Saturday. Keep it simple, keep it intentional, keep it steady, and, above all, keep your focus on the process—not the outcome.

Chapter Lessons:

- Avoid thinking during your swing. Thinking while hitting does not work. Teach yourself to hit the ball with an empty mind.

- Driving ranges, by design, are profit centers (or fun centers).

- Practice should be specifically designed to improve performance.

- Monitor the practice habits of your children, not the outcomes of their swings.

- Random practice and Block practice are different

- Seventy percent of the solution occurs away from your teaching professional.

- Deliberate practice requires deliberate mental attention.

- Deliberate practice will calm down "the noise."

- Your child should be in control of their own practice—they should practice on what they can control.

- Give your child practice tasks they can accomplish. Confidence stems from acquiring skills. Deliberate practice changes movement and ingrains patterns at a cellular level.

- You must test your skills periodically. But, make sure you realize that testing is not practice.

5

OUR INNER DUMMIES

Why do golfers choke? Why does a young junior golfer shoot even par in a practice round and then play worse during the tournament? How can I help my child stay in check emotionally and just play golf? What is happening in my child's brain?

This chapter introduces some key terms of the mental game: The Limbic Brain, Emotional Sabotage, Routine, Inner Dummy and The Path to Anxiety and will give you areas to focus on when you are talking to them about tournament preparation.

We often hear about making each day special or that we should be living for the moment. The truth is that most days are spent in the same basic model. Each evening we are in some type of **rest/relax period** in which we watch a little television, visit with our family and get some sleep. During this period, we generally begin to **assimilate a plan** for the following day. Upon waking, we begin to implement our plan.

Not too long into our day we will be facing a **stimulus** perceived as either negative or positive as it fits into our **plan**. Once the stimulus hits, we get emotional. "Yes! This is exactly what I thought would happen!" Or, "There is no way this could happen right now! C'mon, man!"

Commonly, one of two things happen: we either revert to our **routine** or become **emotionally hijacked**. Businesses have procedures built in to sales or customer service so that when stimulus hits, the employee will have a routine to follow. These procedures keep the employee and customer from being emotionally sabotaged or hijacked.

This cycle of **rest/relax, plan, implementation of plan, stimulus, routine/ or emotional hijacking happens each day.** What does this have to do with junior golf? Well, it is quite simple. Johnny is ready for bed. He played his practice round and is going over a few of the shots he will need to hit tomorrow. A few minutes later, he is asleep. Morning comes and it is time to get ready. The plan starts. On hole number three, a stimulus appears via a missed seven iron and a three putt. Double bogey! Is Johnny going to be emotionally hijacked?

More importantly let's look at Old Johnny. Old Johnny drove his son three hours across the state line for this tournament. He walked with him during the practice round to provide support. At dinner they talked about the tournament and created a plan. (Most likely Old Johnny provided much of the plan.) On the way to the course, he went over a few more strategic tips. The missed seven iron was not part of the plan. "Two over through three holes," Old Johnny thinks to himself.

The round continues. Old Johnny stays with it emotionally until the eighth hole when a three-putt bogey gets Johnny to three over for the tourney. "I am a whole state away from home and this rascal has already blown his chance to win. He is completely out of it before making the turn. Maybe he can birdie the ninth hole and get it back!"

On the ninth hole Johnny hits a less than perfect tee shot that carries to the fairway bunker, hits the cart path and bounds over the white stakes. Old Johnny drops his head, thinking, "You have to be kidding me! Come on son! We went over this yesterday!" Johnny feels humiliated, let down and knows what his father is thinking.

Now, do you think these two are **emotionally hijacked?** Have you been there? I think we have all been there either as players or parents. This behavior is obviously tied to outcome much more than process. The stimulus of the score has emotionally hijacked the pair. When they will get back to routine is not known. It might be on the tenth hole, at dinner, or next week after they get back to the normal daily cycles. But where does this behavior come from?

It comes from the brain. More specifically it comes from the sub neocortex. This area of our brain drives, holds and controls emotional impulses that surge over us like waves. For our purposes, we will call this system the limbic system. This system is different from our rational system. The emotional brain and the rational brain are always competing. The problem with the limbic system, and its drive of the emotional brain, is that it seems to fight rational thinking. Think of the example of Old Johnny and his son. Why can't they see that it is only a golf tournament? Why are they living and dying with every shot? Because their limbic systems are in control.

Core Limbic Drives

There are five core limbic drives. We will start with **sexual drive**. The old saying, "More great players have been lost to perfume, alcohol and gasoline than anything else!" speaks to the power of the limbic drive. Sexual attraction is very easy to identify with and it is exceedingly easy to see those hormones kick in and change our children's actions and behaviors.

Next is our **power drive.** It is the pecking order. It is the reason we don't like people that always seem to beat us. It is the reason we still get that uneasy feeling when someone blows it by us thirty yards off the tee. Taken to excess, it is the source of envy, jealousy or hatred.

Another drive is our **survival drive.** We must live to fight another day. It is also the area where many irrational fears or anxieties surface. If you ever felt like your son or daughter "had" to get the ball in the fairway, you have experienced the survival drive.

Next is the **territorial drive.** Have you ever gotten angry when someone hit your new club? Have you ever felt like it was more difficult or possibly easier to win at your home course? This is part of the enigmatic story of Mr. Hogan in 1953 when he went to the U.S. Open for the first time and won!

Finally, there is a drive that underlies the reason I am writing this book, **nurturance.** It is not likely any of us would deem this drive as undesirable. This drive is the reason we like to form attachments to others, to build relationships, and to be a part of the "herd."

The limbic system is a group of structures in the brain associated with emotions. It is not a stand-alone part of our brain—it is also associated with behavior, learning, smell and long-term memory.

Through the years there have been experiments with lab rats that manipulated the limbic system's four main structures: the amygdala, the hippocampus, the limbic cortex and the septal area. A relevant experiment was published in 1954 when researchers (Olds and Milner) placed electrodes into rats' limbic systems. Each time a rat pressed on a certain lever, the researchers would stimulate the rat's limbic system. The rats ignored food or water and died from exhaustion from continuously pressing on the lever. When areas of the limbic system were removed from the test animals, they became tame.

You, the parent, must understand that your child's brain is not so much different than your own. You and your child will always be emotional creatures. In fact, it is this limbic system of drives that can be either harnessed (and helpful) or unfettered (and harmful).

Let's go back to Johnny. When he completed the round, his score was 80! While he is obviously emotionally upset, he searches for something to default to so that he can quiet down the limbic system. Old Johnny has been emotionally sabotaged for going on three hours now. He also senses a need for some emotional tranquility. What do they do?

Should Johnny go hit balls? Should Old Johnny go hit the bar? Should Johnny eat and rest? Should Old Johnny kick in the power drive and jump down his son's throat? **Emotional sabotage is so difficult because anxiety is possible everywhere at golf tournaments!**

Both young and Old Johnny will return to rest and relax. They will both formulate a different plan. They will both implement the plan and a stimulus will appear. When it does, the limbic system will kick in once more. The sad part is two-fold. First, if the outcome of winning the tournament is the primary focus, neither Johnny can avoid being emotionally sabotaged. Secondly, they will both see "emotion" as the problem and will probably waste considerable mental energy trying to "feel" positive.

Placing your emphasis on winning is not only wrong—it's disastrous. Golf is a game of variables. Each hole is different, each putt is different, in length and break, each day the wind is different. The list can go on and on. One thing is certain: the variables are what make the game difficult. If every hole looked the same and the conditions were always the same, golf would be (relatively) easy. If you want to experience considerable failure at golf, teach your children (or yourself) to be an additional variable in this game of variables.

How do you, the parent, protect yourself from being emotionally sabotaged? **Begin by placing your emphasis on going back to the learned and practiced routine, not on outcome.**

Mental Toughness

Similarly, your junior golfer can get through the variables the game presents if they have a protocol. In golf, we call protocol "our routine." Place your emphasis on your child going through their routine on each shot and you are giving your child a chance to minimize the impact of the variables the game presents.

I think of "mental toughness" as being "mentally defined." Golfers on the path to success know what they can control on the course. Parents also know what their child can control. Both the child and the parent know that the only thing they can control is getting committed to the shot and hitting it with the same physical and mental protocol each time.

Defining your physical and mental protocol is a major topic in sports psychology. **Emotional sabotage will not occur if the only goal of each shot on each hole during each round is to run through a mental and physical routine.** The routine is specific, constant and the child has control. Will your child still get angry over the results of a shot? Sure. Any competitor will. Will you still get let down by the results? Sure. The backbone of success is failure. The key is to channel anger at failure into an even more dedicated focus on routine

Having a great routine will not lead to lower scores and better shots immediately. Defining the routines used in the full swing, short game and putting is the first step. Practicing these routines is the second step. Successfully integrating these routines during tournament play is the third step. Along the way you will still see bad shots and scores that upset you, but your child is on the path to minimizing possible errors.

You must realize that improvement comes through a process of elimination. By defining a routine and defining the child's primary focus on the course, the mind will not be the reason for poor performance. The greatest power of the physical and mental routine on the course is ruling out the mind as the source of mistakes. Golf swings and bodies can be fixed as long as the mind is a constant. I really have no answers for players whose minds are a variable. In these cases, players are easy targets for emotional hijackings. My experience tells me an emotionally hijacked player cannot be fixed.

Initially, understand the physical and mental routines are the key to eliminating mental mistakes on the course. By signaling the routine the same way each time and having the same number of looks (each one should have a purpose) the player will be choosing to be a constant in a game of variables. **Once the routine has been practiced and has become the primary focus, there will be much less emotional sabotaged for players and the parents of players.**

The parent will memorize the routine and know when something changes. All you can ask of your children is to prepare correctly and then go out and run their routine on each shot. If their golf swing does not perform, they will still miss shots. If their bodies are dysfunctional, they will still miss shots. If their strategy is incorrect, they will still miss shots. If their green reading skills are poor, they will still miss putts. Thankfully, golf swings, bodies, strategies and green reading skill can all be fixed in the presence of a routine. Asking your child to concentrate on a routine is giving them a task they can control. Asking (or expecting) them to win tournament is insanity that almost always leads to emotional disasters.

Science tells us this about emotion: emotion sharpens our skills to a point, but when too much emotion appears, our skills cannot be used. **Attempting to mitigate emotion on the course is wasted effort.** If there is too much emotion, the process is not the primary focus. By keeping the focus on performing the physical and mental routine, emotions will be kept in check. However, I see so many parents say, "My son/daughter just doesn't have it up here!" Hogwash! These parents are ones who believe the level of mental skills cannot grow. If the primary goal is something attainable on each shot, then emotions will not run too high. **The truth is that when emotions run too high, the outcome has become the primary focus.**

When I was a kid my father would time my routine. We didn't really know what a routine did; we just knew that routines were in all the golf magazines. We came up with twenty-two seconds as the time of my routine. The only problem was that I loved playing golf with the men's group at our club. A twenty-two second routine stuck out like a sore thumb among a bunch of guys that played eighteen holes in three hours. So as soon as my father caught me not going through my timed routine, he became emotionally hijacked. I was probably twelve or thirteen, but I remember the lecture he gave me riding from the sixth green to the seventh tee. The choices boiled down to either go play by myself and run my routine or continue to play with the guys and deep-six the routine. Of course, I chose the men's group.

My father and I had it wrong. A routine does not take twenty-two seconds. Adding to a routine just to add it is the opposite of why we have a routine. The goal is to get the conscious mind involved in a step-by-step process that allows the subconscious skill of the player to appear repeatedly. The goal is for the step- by-step process to be the primary focus, so the limbic system doesn't kick in and turn our perfectly functioning driving range swing into a collection of lurches on the golf course.

Routines and Pre-Shot Routines

Look at it this way. Suppose concentrating on the target is our true goal. Therefore, we need a routine to achieve this goal. So, running our routine is now our goal. The goal of concentrating on the target can be viewed as a by-product of running the routine. When a player is really just playing golf and concentrating on the target, they will do the same thing each time. Think of what happens to that same player when more variables are added (like a tournament, trophies, stature in the club, adulation of peers, etc.). Adding these variables to the outcome will likely lead the player to perceive that the shot is more than just a shot. Now if the routine is not defined, then what does the player make as the primary focus of the shot? The routine or the outcome? Most likely, it is the outcome, which has a negative effect of the actual outcome. By making routine the primary focus, the player maximizes the likelihood of a good outcome.

A typical routine starts with a physical signal, such as tugging on the shirt or putting both hands on the club. The routine might proceed looking at the target for alignment as you set up to the ball. From there it continues with a confirmation look at the target and proceeding to swing. It is quite simple and fast (eight to thirteen seconds on average):

- Physical signa
- 1st look for alignment
- 2nd look to confirm the target

- Go!

By contrast, my father and I were building an elaborate routine that involved practice swings, strategy, breaths, looks, etc. Our mistake was very common: **we thought a good routine had to be an elaborate routine.** Building a routine will probably take more than an hour, but not much. Just video your child on the course and ask them why they are doing what they are doing. Define why they are looking at the target. Define the physical signal at the beginning of the routine. Then, make a video your child going through the newly defined routine. Talk about how concentrating on this routine results in the best shot given the variables that they cannot control

Pre-shot routines are different from the routine we have been discussing. Pre- shot routines involve strategy, practice swings and decision making. **These practice swings and decisions are not part of your routine because a pre-shot routine is not constant—it can be unique to each shot.** For example, if I am faced with an easy chip shot, I might not even take a practice swing. If my ball is buried four inches deep in Bermuda grass, I might need to take five practice swings to get committed to the shot. The point is that you **must understand that a pre-shot routine and the routine are different**

My guess is that most people do not understand this distinction. They think that playing golf with a routine slows them down. Quite the opposite is true. As a general rule, people take ages over the golf ball before they swing. They make a decision on the club (or the line of the putt) rather quickly, then they walk up to the ball and turn on their minds! This process is the opposite of a routine. Figure out the shot and rehearse your swing if you want. When you are committed to the shot, think of nothing but your routine. For example: physical signal, first look for alignment, second look to confirm target, and go! Do you see the difference between a typical process and what is a constant routine?

Choking

I really do not think choking exists. Of course, we have all felt our brains switch gears. We have all felt (note: feeling is an emotion) when this shot or this putt was really important. What do we perceive? We perceive the outcome. We perceive that if this crucial putt falls, we will be closer to our desired outcome. Do you see how the outcome is now your focus? If the outcome becomes your primary focus, your limbic system sees its chance to "do its dance." A mixture of neurons, synapses, nerves, chemicals and different areas of the brain ignite and a system as old as the human race kicks in. Now you are aware! The small appendages begin to shake as adrenaline kicks in. On the outside we look normal; on the inside we are churning.

Does this sound like a recipe for choking? Well it is not. It is normal. Every great athlete will tell you (after they are retired) they went through this same set of events. They knew that they were only in control of the process. They defaulted to the series of events they could control. As you should be thinking by now, a focus on what you can control is a routine. **Simply stated, choking is really just being emotionally sabotaged.** The inner dummy is fully on display for public viewing, and the limbic system is doing a sack dance over the poor outcome.

All golfers must understand how they can easily become emotionally sabotaged. The way the brain and mind fight one another is the way we are all made. All those voices you hear over a putt? Limbic System. That feeling of total loss of motor control? Limbic System. It is your inner dummy struggling to escape because a stimulus has appeared. You are at the crossroads between becoming emotionally hijacked and regaining control. The road to regaining control is to make the running of your routine your primary focus.

Every young golfer will benefit greatly from a parent who is knowledgeable in the ways of a routine. A deep and unshakable belief in keeping the process the primary objective is necessary to attain your goals. Defaulting to the routine is a learned skill. The parent must "buck the system" and grade the performance by how well their entrant followed the routine throughout the tournament. The score is secondary to the routine. When your children understand and buys into the notion that running the routine is the primary objective, choking will disappear.

The conscious mind becomes aware of emotions after the emotions have begun. Emotions literally take place before conscious awareness. Part of your child's brain (or yours) is beginning a **process of appraisal** that sets emotion in motion before the conscious mind has a chance. Our brains are constantly appraising situations on a subconscious level.

I remember a young student of mine who went on to a superb college to play Division 1 golf. He was a state high school and state junior champion. He had good skills and understood the game. After a delightful first year it was time to take it to the next level. Enter sports psychologist. One spring day he came up to do some work on his game and discuss his play. He wasn't getting much out of his game and, by all appearances, he was in a slump. The golf swing was in order. The ball flight was in order. The pitching and putting motions were in order. I was a bit perplexed, so we decided to go out on the course.

Because I had known him since he was a youngster and had played several rounds with him, I had a feel for his pace of play. What I found on the course was a different player. He was standing behind the ball. Visualizing the shot, I assume.

The routine was long, with practice swings and deep breaths. I asked him what he was doing during this seemingly endless period before hitting the ball. "Trying to wipe the slate clean," was his remark. I went on to identify this as meaning trying to get rid of any negative emotion before embarking on the shot.

Do you understand what he was doing? He was trying to get rid of emotions through his conscious, rational mind. He was trying to stop them. The only problem was they were forming before he even realized it. **Trying to become a machine that hits every shot with the perfect amount of emotion is not the aim of a routine.** Emotions will flare up on their own as your child gets closer or further from the goal. The goal of a routine is to run the routine and let the outcome take care of itself.

This type of thinking sits neatly on shelf along with deliberate practice and functional training. This type of thinking has little in common with ball beating and early specialization. Children are inherently smart. They know when they are pushing themselves to learn. They know when they are pushing their bodies to move better. It will be difficult for the child who does not practice with intention to then make a routine primary on the course. It will be very difficult for the aspiring college player, who has specialized in golf starting at age eleven, to make the process primary.

The limbic system has been called "the devil's playground." My father referred to it as the "mental midget." Whatever you wish to call the limbic system is fine. Sometimes I refer to it as "the genius" in a rather sarcastic tone. What you must understand is the limbic system is not your child. It is part of your child, just as it is part of you. It has been passed down through generations of human civilization via DNA. Everyone from Jack Nicklaus to your child has battled his or her inner dummies. It happens on the baseball field, the soccer field and in NASCAR

I recently had the opportunity to sit down with one of the most renowned sport psychologists of our era. He has worked with professional and collegiate players on a variety of levels and in a variety of sports. One of his best stories revolved around a NASCAR driver who came to him to improve his performance.

"After a little conversation I asked him how I could help," the doc said. "Well doc," the racer said, "I am not scared. Being scared won't get you past the dirt track circuit. But there is this one thing...."

"Go on." The doc said.

"Well at 185 mph this #3 car (Dale Earnhardt) will get inches from my rear bumper. Then he will start tapping his index finger on the top of steering wheel motioning for me to get over or else. I am having a tough time getting that out of my mind."

Anxiety

Why is it that golf seems to breed fear, anxiety and will make a player "play scared?" As children we may have played aggressive sports and felt a turning in our stomachs and a rush of adrenaline. Every time I see a picture of Eddy Vedder stage diving into a sea of people, I think of boxing. That is really what it felt like. Once the bell sounds to start the bout, you were in the air. Seconds later, you were out of breath and could feel the punches landing. I have heard a similar account when people talk about playing football. The anxiety leaves when the buzzer sounds

But it is often not that way in golf. Often times our children and ourselves cannot shake the anxiety. Before you label yourself or your children as people who don't have the mental make-up to be a great champion, let's look at why this happens.

First there must be some sort of emotion creating *worry*. *Worrying* about score or what other players will think of you, for example. For *worry* to grow, there must be some sign that it could happen to you and there must be a substantial amount of time for you to find out if it will. We have all seen the expression on the faces of junior golfers as Roy (who made a nine on #7) recounts his adventure through bunkers, trees, deep grass and finally into the hole. On the PGA Tour, when this type of talk starts up players will absolutely walk off. It is like a plague. Who wants to catch the plague?

With time for the *worry* to grow, all we need now are three simple mental steps.

1. *Imagine yourself doing it.* Just take a second to see you topping it in the creek on #7.

2. *Imagine yourself not doing that at all. In fact, fight the emotion by telling yourself it is impossible for that to happen to you.* This takes a little self-talk. You must fight the emotion with another emotional voice from your limbic system. *3) Try to figure out a way to avoid that shot.* Now we have *Anxiety!* Not only that, we have at least a couple of hours before we get to the 7th hole so there is plenty of time for it to really creep into our emotions.

If the child's job is to run their physical/mental routine and that is the primary objective, do you think there will be room for emotion to grow? The type of worry we outline is totally outcome oriented.

For *anxiety* to set in, the child has to see himself making the mistake. They will do so, I assure you. All it takes for anxiety to emerge is a second of visualization. They will try the second visual also—but this process is wasted mental energy. Fighting an emotion with another emotion is simply a losing proposition. You are much better off ignoring the emotional voice. When routine is primary, the emotional voice can be bagged up. So finally, the child needs to figure out a way to prevent anxiety from happening. Anxiety appears in the form of stomach aches, complaints about tournament golf and sudden injuries.

Step back and look at the picture clearly. The child has either not been taught a routine or has not practiced it enough. They are still clutching the "outcome." It is the parent's and coach's job to get into that child's mind and change their mind-set. Parents are seventy percent of the recipe. It is not that children don't have the mental aptitude for golf; it is they don't have the mental training for a sport consisting of so many subtle variables and one that takes so much time to practice and play.

The Limbic System + Time + Fighting The Emotion + A Lack Of Proper Preparation + The Outcome Being Primary = An Inner Dummies Riot!

This is the true equation for those children who cannot get over the hump of competitive golf because they get emotionally hijacked on the course. Parents of these players can usually be spotted pacing the cart paths, biting their fingernails and kicking trees. Living and dying with each shot, these parents are emotionally hijacked.

The Limbic System + Time + Ignoring the voice of the emotion + Proper Preparation + The Routine Being Primary = A Champion's Mind.

This equation summarizes where "the best" hang out. They don't fight the emotion. They don't have some special inner being who is taking emotion and throwing it out the window of their biological body. They are simply concerned with doing their best, and their best is taking care of what they can take care of: getting in tune with the target and hitting the shot.

Chapter Lessons:

- Understand the Daily Cycle.

- The Limbic System has five basic Drives.

- Emotional Sabotage will happen—just understand what it is and how to overcome it.

- The Mental/Physical Routine is the key to eliminating mental mistakes on the course. Your child may still make strategic, mechanical or physical mistakes on the course.

- Floating Anxiety is a sign of being Emotionally Hijacked.

- Attempting to mitigate emotion on the course is a waste of mental energy.

- An elaborate routine may not be a good routine.

- Choking exists only when a person is emotionally sabotaged.

- Trying to hit shots with the perfect amount of emotion on each shot is not the aim of a routine.

- Worry turns into Anxiety because the outcome is the primary objective.

- Create an equation that gives your child the best chance of becoming great. Then, practice it.

6

THE BEGINING

The drama of the major professional golf tours plays out on nearly thirty Sundays each year. On many, if not most of those afternoons, golf fans around the world can follow the drama down to the wire thanks to television, internet and radio. There is a big payout for those that find themselves victorious due to a combination of strategy, talent and sometimes due to another's lack of those abilities on a given day.

With the winner's share at 18% of the total purse, golf is one of the most capitalistic of sports. While often times the difference between first and tenth may be only a few strokes, the tenth-place finisher will receive only 2.7% of the payout breakdown, six times less than the victor. Adding to the drama is the thirty-six-hole cut, where the top seventy players (including ties) continue to play the weekend while the other eighty plus players have the weekend off. The last place finisher of the tournament receives 0.2% of the total purse.

With the average purse on the PGA Tour roughly $6.5 million, the LPGA Tour $1.5 million, the Web.com Tour $710,000 and the Symetra Tour (LPGA'S version of Web.com Tour) roughly $150,000, there is a premium on getting to the "big tour."

Decades before the drama unfolds on the major tours, the drama of tour school begins as the stars of today hone their game. All golfers, upon turning professional, are independent contractors. It doesn't matter if a golfer is ranked the number one thousand or the number one amateur in the world, they will not be drafted by a major tour to come and play. No one, absolutely no one, is given a PGA or LPGA Tour card because of their amateur resumé; they have to earn it.

A very small percentage will get sponsor's exemptions into tournaments on a major tour and perform well enough to earn their card for the year. While the U.S. Open and British Open tournaments host open qualifiers that allow anyone to sign up and play their way into the event, the only way to get on a major tour is through tour school. For many years, The "school" was held in three separate stages. At each stage the top twenty-five or so players (including ties) move on. At final stage the actual amount of cards given out varied from 25-50 players.

During the LPGA Finals of 2018 the top twenty players got their LPGA Tour card. During the Web.com Tour Finals of 2018 the top twenty five players received their Web.com Tour card combined with the Top 25 from the current years money list. Those finishing outside "the number" at finals earn a conditional status that provides a possible spot in one or more of the tournaments. Getting to the final stage of tour school and finishing one shot behind the cutoff illustrates the capitalistic nature of the sport. Those that do not earn a spot at the finals go to the "mini tours."

The mini tours may not have any or very little corporate sponsorships, so the entry fees of the tournament contestants contribute the purse amount. While the purse amounts can be in the $200,000 range, they boast a much higher entry fee and larger playing fields. Some have called it a "proving ground" and others "legalized gambling" but either way the check for a second-place finish on the PGA Tour and the Mini Tour will be many zeros apart. The road to either position can simply be the difference between a shot made here and a shot lost there.

The finals of the Web.com Tour of 2018 was contested over three stages and then to the finals. At the end only a few shots separated a fully exempt card from the last of the conditional status cards earned. Therefore, a player five shots out of 10th place will have much less status than a player two, three, or four shots out of 10th place. He will be fortunate to get into three to five events. Those finishing seven to nine shots back of the 10th place finisher, will play a full schedule of mini tours.

It is capitalistic. Good play at the right time will take care of itself and golfers leaving their amateur careers behind know the reality of tour school and earning their spot on the major tours. It is part of the allure of the game and a part of what makes the drama so emotional for the champions on those thirty or so Sunday afternoons. For some, only two or three years earlier they were on the outside looking in. It also builds drama inside the tour, with some players knowing if their poor play continues they may lose their position on the major tour.

In 1983 Jim Gallagher, Jr. was on the outside looking in. Upon graduating from the University of Tennessee in the spring, Jim attended tour school in the fall at TPC Sawgrass in Jacksonville, Florida, and earned a coveted spot in that third and final stage.

As Jim is heading into the finals of tour school, it is important to understand there is one major tour where money can be made, the PGA Tour. At Sawgrass, the field of PGA Tour Qualifying School consisted of 144 players and there were fifty spots up for grabs. The now famous TPC Sawgrass had only been open for three years. "We had all heard the horror stories about how difficult it was, all the sand, the 17th green and all the rest the course had in store for us. Sprinkle in tour finals and it was going to be tough." Jim recalled. Jim's caddy happened to be the same caddie Craig Stadler had on the bag during his only major victory, the 1982 Masters. Sounds promising, right?

However, 1982 was also the last year Augusta National required the players to use caddies from the club. Caddying for Craig Stadler during his major win didn't necessarily mean he was of great character. Jim recalls the week, "It was a long week with four practice rounds and six rounds of competition. The caddies weren't making a bunch of money back then; a lot of them wanted to be paid in advance. As a player you never wanted to pay them in advance because they may not show up. You have to remember that at this time I didn't have a relationship with the caddy; we all just went by what other players and caddies said.

"Going into the fifth round the caddy shows up late. Not late for the warm up but actually late for the tee time. At that point I had paid him enough to be even for the week and my dad was standing off number one tee watching and listening to our conversation just before I teed off. As I recall my dad said something about 'forgetting more about caddying than you would ever know' and he caddied for me the final two rounds."

After a rain out and thirty-six holes, Willie Wood would medal at the 1983 PGA Tour Finals. There were fifty-seven PGA Tour cards given out at the end of the tournament and Jim Gallagher, Jr. was now a member of the PGA Tour. Jim recalls, "After all the hard work put in the years before and how furious me and my dad were after the caddy not showing up, I just remember my dad grabbing the reigns as a caddy and the two of us getting through it. It was emotional to say the least.

For me, at that point in my life, that was my greatest accomplishment. I had always dreamt of being on the PGA Tour and now I finally was. All the hard work that I had put in and all the years my parents had given me the opportunity to follow this dream had finally been realized

"I was a good junior golfer and I was a good collegiate golfer. I always thought I was better than I was given credit for. There are politics in junior golf and there are politics in collegiate golf. Therefore, earning my spot on the PGA Tour proved to me that I could play with the best."

There is a pecking order on the PGA Tour. The players refer to it as the "re-shuffle" and "categories." The PGA Tour refers to it as the Player Eligibility Rankings. Today there are roughly thirty-seven different categories ranging from the winners of a major championship to the top finishers on the Web.com Tour. This creates another world inside the world of the tour, the reality that if you are a rookie, you had better play well early and move up the rankings.

Jim would soon discover what those before him and those after him realize; just because you are a card-carrying member of the PGA Tour doesn't mean you will get in the event. As a coach I can tell you how daunting it is to work with players in the category. They feel a sense of accomplishment when the card comes in the mail, as they should. Then they are anxious to play well immediately. That means they often go through the trial by fire, being ball flight and score conscious **all the time!** The stimulus of "feeling as if you have made it" and the reality that "you are not there yet" can throw the best of us into an emotional frenzy. Jim Jr. was heading there.

"I realized the dream of the PGA Tour but pretty soon I also realized that I had finished around 30th at the finals and started to wonder just how many tournaments I would actually get into. A few months after earning my tour card, I find myself writing letters to tournament committees to try and get in events.

"The first event was at Torrey Pines in San Diego. A good friend of mine, Peter Kiley, was a college student at the University of San Diego and he caddied for me. The first two days I shoot 70, 70, which was four under par. I miss the cut by a shot. I was like 'Wow! These guys are really good.'

"That was my intro into the tour. I was proud of my 70,70 but was scratching my head about missing the cut. I mean what the heck! Could the golf have been better? Yes, but it wasn't what I would have called 'bad' either. I got in the Bing Crosby Clambake due to a friendship with Nathaniel Crosby, so I had my second event there at Pebble Beach. Unfortunately, I didn't play well and missed that cut. Believe it or not, that was it on the West Coast."

The "West Coast Swing" is a group of tournaments played in the Western States. Rich in history and tradition, this group includes: PGA West TPC Stadium Course, Torrey Pines, TPC Scottsdale, Pebble Beach and Riviera Country Club. In the early years of the PGA Tour all the players went West, following the sun to get away from the cold winters during late January and February. For those searching to move up on the priority rankings on the PGA Tour, good play or poor play will make a dramatic difference in their position by March. Poor play from a rookie while on the West Coast will have a dramatic effect to what they get into by early spring

Behind the scenes there is more going on. It is so easy for the flow of performance to drop and the emotions of the player to fall. Each week there are roughly 144 guys playing in the PGA Tour event. That means 144 caddies. It also means another fifty equipment reps, tour officials, rules officials, etc. This equates to a world of just over three hundred people who travel town-to-town putting on exhibitions in scoring and performance for the fans. There are low numbers, really low numbers and mind-blowing shots that "no one in the gallery has ever seen." Everyday someone hits a drive, chip and putt that is world class. Everyone is good and everyone is chasing that same thing: winning. To win out there you have to play some of your very best golf over four days. This literally creates a culture of improvement, innovation and pushing the limits of what a human can do with a golf ball.

To the outsider it is hard to understand. It looks like the guys on the PGA Tour are under so much stress and pressure. On the inside it is much different. There is a kindred spirit floating around those guys, especially among those who don't have to worry about their status to get into tournaments. That culture breeds flow and exceptional performance in a way that cannot be created without it. For Jim, he was not a part of that culture just yet. He was on the outside looking in. That is a difficult spot for the golfer and a coach.

"Here I am finishing in the high twenties at tour school and getting in two tournaments during the first month or so of the season," Jimmy remembers. "At the LA Open that year I was seventh alternate. Not thinking I was going to get in I went to the airport to fly out instead of going to the golf course. Lo and behold they played one guy short that week so I would have gotten in. Had I gone and sat on the first tee I would have gotten in. After the West Coast Swing there was a re-shuffle and I got pushed back to the mid-to-high forties so my eligibility ranking was going the wrong way. This dream of mine was turning into a nightmare

"The Florida Swing was coming up after the re-shuffle and I knew I wasn't going to get in any of the tournaments because of my number. So I decide I am going to Monday and qualify for each event that I can. At Doral I qualified for the event. Then I make my first cut. I don't get in the next week at Honda but learning from the LA Open, I sat on the first tee and waited but with no luck.

For the entire month of March, the PGA Tour makes it home in Florida. PGA National in West Palm Beach, Doral in Miami, Innisbrook in Palm Harbor and Bay Hill in Orlando make up the tournament sites. If a prominent player did not make it out during the West Coast Swing (which is doubtful) they will certainly be on site for each of these events. The reason is simple, during that second week of April a small tournament in Augusta, Georgia, will be held. The best of the best on the PGA Tour will be shaking rust off and fine-tuning through this stretch for their shot at the green jacket.

"During all my off weeks in Florida I am paying $3.00 or $4.00 for a bucket of balls and $27.00 to play PGA National. I didn't have access to the tournament practice facilities unless I was in the tournament. So, I am basically a mini-tour player with a PGA Tour card at this point. I remember thinking 'This is crazy!'"

Grit. A word that means so much and is tough sometimes to even define. If you are looking for a place to understand Jim Gallagher Jr. on the inside look right here. He is at PGA National paying for range balls. The Tour and maybe more importantly the feeling of belonging and accomplishment is very far away. He probably can't remember what his golf ball was doing back then during those lonely practice sessions. Whatever amount of grit that he had was growing. His love of the game and desire to win and compete was etched inside his heart. Giving up was not even a thought. Jim Jr. was growing up. He was building the character, the drive and the internal fortitude the world would later see.

The only trouble with these types of days, weeks and years in our own lives is we can't see it. We don't have a crystal ball that shows us the future. It is much easier to see looking back and at this point in his life Jim would need a lot of encouragement from his family and friends. This encouragement would also have to come from ball flight and performance.

"During the Florida swing I try "to Monday" for a couple other events but don't get in. At this point it is basically April and The Masters is coming up so all the players with more status than me are getting out and shaking the rust off before heading to Augusta. I am making no progress at all and more importantly I am not making any money. I have friends that are letting me stay with them and taking care of me. It was just a bunch of sitting around and driving around the country.

"Through April of that year I had played in three events. At the Houston Open that year I finally get in on my number again. That is where the infamous meeting of all the '83 grads of tour school met with the PGA Policy Board and complained about access to tournaments. Jim Colbert stood up and said, 'Boys this will solve all your problems: JUST PLAY BETTER.' Colbert was a member of the Policy Board and his statement crawled all over us. But as a fifty-eight-year-old man now, I can say Colbert was right. If you play well on tour it takes care of everything."

A part of the PGA Tour that is reality is the notion of either being one of the boys or not one of the boys. It is similar to being on the roster in a team sport but not seeing the field but twenty percent of the time. Great play is celebrated first by the players and their family. It continues with the media and the fans, but it is also celebrated by all those around the traveling host of entities that revolve around the PGA Tour. Those entities are caddies, instructors, equipment manufacturers and any type of aid that "may have been" a part of the great performance.

Being a "part" of the PGA Tour and being a "member" of the PGA Tour are very different. One may be issued a card as being a "member" of the PGA Tour with "ALL ACCESS" on it, but that doesn't mean the player will really feel like a true "member." Membership comes when there is great play, that spotlight proved by play worthy of celebration.

For most of the players on the PGA Tour this is a normal inclusion. Each level of golf beginning with junior and collegiate golf carries this same level of true membership. As with most high school and collegiate teams, there will only be "five travel" players who represent their schools at tournaments. Mini tours have the same level of membership as those who travel together over the years to create their own groups of friendships.

Do not discount the drive for membership when it comes to performance. This need to be a part of the inner circle is challenging and skills must be proven. This "membership" carries with it an elixir of chemical cocktails our brain releases that is second to none.

Behind the scenes is a coach and a father stepping in to encourage and remind Jim of his ability. I can assure you Senior was commenting on how great Junior is swinging it. Senior is reminding Jim Jr. of how great of a pitcher and chipper he is. Jim's past accomplishments are also serving him greatly right now: winning the Indiana State Am and State Open in the same year, a four-year letterman at Tennessee, and a near win at a national junior event as a teen. Deep inside Jim knows he is a "member" and he is hungry to prove it.

Golf, at least at the professional level, is not completely cut throat. I have witnessed many an "elder" of the PGA Tour take the time to get to know a rookie and many great relationships begin in this way. On tour there are different courses, different strategies, different hotels and places to eat. Even the navigation of airports and rental cars can be a learning curve for the rookie. The rookies, or even the second- or third-year guys who have been struggling a bit to make their mark on the PGA Tour and feel like a true "member" are often times helped tremendously by a household name offering a few kind words of encouragement. Understanding this can help you put into context how the rookies of '83 felt during Colbert's remarks.

"I got in Dallas late in May and a few more events through the summer/fall. Then if you finished 126th – 150th on the PGA Tour Money list you got a conditional card and got an exemption to the finals of tour school. So, as I got in a few more events through the summer my new goal was just to finish somewhere between 126th and 150th on the money list. I finished 148th on the money list in '84. That got me in the finals of tour school at PGA WEST in Palm Springs. For my rookie season on The PGA Tour I lose money.

"At the '85 tour school that year the Santa Anta winds come up and the wind is blowing at 40 to 50 miles per hour. The guys playing the Dunes Course couldn't get over the water at the 10th hole so the tour called that round off. I missed getting my tour card by one or two shots. So now I have to decide what I am going to do.

"Finishing the '84 season between 126th and 150th on the money list meant I would get in six or eight PGA Tour events during the '85 season. This probably wasn't going to be enough events to keep my card and I couldn't afford to travel around the country Monday qualifying and waiting on tees to see if I got in the tournament.

"The PGA Tour, at that time, had what they called the Tournament Player's Series. It was the precursor to what is now the Web.com Tour. The Tournament Player's Series was six events and the leading money winner would get their PGA Tour card for the following year. I went to play the Tournament Series that year and I won in Hattiesburg. The Tournament Player's Series at Hattiesburg Country Club was played opposite The Master's that year.

"In 1985, on the first playoff hole, I beat Paul Azinger to win the Magnolia Classic in a rain shortened 36-hole event and won $27,000. Because of my eligibility ranking I also started getting in a few PGA Tour events. That $27,000 I won was more than I made in the 1984 season.

"In Albuquerque, New Mexico, I win another one. On the last hole I make a thirty-five footer to beat Kenny Perry by a shot. Kenny would probably tell you it was a hundred-footer! So that gave me two wins and propelled me to the leading money winner of the Tournament Player's Series. I had to make a decision because I was playing well. I decided to focus on the remainder of the Tournament Player's Series and at the end of that year I was the leading money winner and had full exemption for the '86 season on The PGA Tour."

As a coach I remind players all the time that practice pays off later. I remind them sticking to a process that is defined and steady will give them their best chance of accomplishing their goals. In the middle of all this is a lot of calculated, deliberate practice and coaching.

The biggest thing players and coaches wrestle with during the period between sound practice and accomplishment is emotion. The sting of emotion from the reality of not "being there" yet and the burning desire to "get there." In the end, if it is God's will and the player, coach and team can stay on task there will be accomplishment. Listen to Jimmy's account of the "feeling" here.

"A couple of things happened that '85 year. For the first time in two years I actually made some money that was important. Maybe more importantly was that I won on a level that I had not won on before. When I won that event, I was a winner of a professional event and that was a very good feeling. Certainly, the best feeling since getting my tour card in the winter of '83."

Jim Jr. is giving us insight here into the emotional aspects of extraordinary performances. It is a feeling. It is a desire. **Proverbs 12 says: Hope deferred make the heart sick, but desire fulfilled is a tree of life.** Jim's hope of playing the PGA Tour full time in 1984 was deferred. At tour school for the '85 season Jim's hope was deferred. Now in the '85 season Jim Jr., playing the Tournament Player's Tour, has his desire fulfilled. Fulfillment of desire usually brings with it "membership" and Jim was about to experience this membership in so many exciting ways.

Heading into that 1986 year, Jim Gallagher, Jr. received some help from the best in the game, Jack Nicklaus. Jim knew Jackie, Jack Nicklaus's son, from junior golf and Jack extended playing privileges to Jim at Frenchman's Creek Golf Club in Palm Beach Gardens. (Prior to this Jim really didn't have a home course to play and practice.) The access to the golf course was a game changer. Jim Gallagher Jr. got better at golf by playing golf.

Fully exempt and coming off two professional wins, Jim played in thirty-six PGA Tour Events during his '86 campaign. Finishing the year with close to $80,000 in prize money, Jimmy kept his card and, in his own words, "Everything was good." One of the highlights of the year was Jimmy being paired with Nicklaus at Doral. Jack Nicklaus would win his eighteenth and final major championship in April of that same year.

"That tournament was in March and Nicklaus was hitting it terrible at Doral. But boy could he roll because even though he was hitting it terrible he still made the cut. Everything you read about good players being able to get it around the course, even if they don't have their A game is true. Nicklaus had his C game and still beat half the field."

In the terms of membership, feelings, emotion and being a part of something special, Jack Nicklaus was the president of the company at this point. His record over the previous two and a half decades was beyond this world, a seventeen- time major champion. Fame and fortune, along with respect and admiration greeted him each time he stepped on the course. A Nicklaus '86 Master Championship win was somewhat expected.

The reality was that Nicklaus had played in just seven events prior to the '86 Masters. Jack was five years removed from his last major championship.

He was forty-six years old and had back problems. If Nicklaus finished second or missed the cut that week it would not have really affected him financially nor would it have changed the minds of those who admired or supported him. He had proven to himself and the world that he was one of the greatest players to have ever played the game.

Tom McCollister wrote a column in the Atlanta Journal that read: "Nicklaus is gone, done. He just doesn't have the game anymore. It's rusted from the lack of use. He's forty-six and nobody that old wins the Masters." Tom was basically telling Jack that he was no longer a "member" and that can really motivate a human being. That week Nicklaus's son was on the bag and his family there to encourage him. All of the elements were needed for Nicklaus create a magical moment on the back nine of Augusta that April Sunday.

Jack Nicklaus entered that last round T-9th and four shots off the leader Greg Norman. A birdie on the 9th, 10th, and another at 11 and then a bogey at the 12th hole. Nicklaus would play 13 – 16 four under par including a mind blowing 6 iron into the green at the 16th hole that seemed destined to go in when he hit it. The famous picture of Nicklaus came from the 17th green as he birdied the 71st hole of the tournament. The par on 18 gave Jack Nicklaus the Masters Championship for the sixth time.

We will never know what would have happened without Tom writing that column. We will never know what would have happened without Jack's son on the bag. What we do know is that day did not just happen. There were years of training as a youngster by Jack Grout, there was a U.S. Open that in Ben Hogan's words he "should have one" and we must remember the first tournament Jack won as a professional was the U.S. Open. There were junior tournaments played all over the country, college golf, and amateur tournaments of course. Jack had won on every level and Jack had become a "member" of course. He had rubbed shoulders and learned and defeated the biggest names in the game. Jack Nicklaus and his decades of preparation only needed to be invited into the "flow" and by all respects being told he was old and washed up did the trick.

Jim Gallagher, Jr., at the same time was a member and he was not shy in getting to know the best in the game. Someone had encouraged him get in there with the veterans and get to know the game they played. Someone had also encouraged him that he could get in there with them and battle it out. That someone could have been a number of people, including and possibly most importantly, himself.

"In 1986 I started playing practice rounds with Bruce Lietzke. I met him in '84 but I played as many practice rounds as I could with him. By simply playing with him I started hitting more fades to copy his ball flight. My goals those first couple of years was to be paired with as many good players as possible and to beat them. In my mind I wanted to prove to them that I could really play.

"There is no better compliment than when you get through playing with a Raymond Floyd, Jack Nicklaus, JC Snead or any of those top players and they say, 'You are going to be a helluva player.' I was just driven to try to prove to everyone, including myself, that I was one of the best players. By watching these top players, I slowly began to believe I could do it. I was in awe of these guys like Arnold Palmer and Johnny Miller but when I was on that course with them, I was trying to beat them. From '83 to '86 I was growing as a player because I was around these guys.

"I don't know I ever paid attention to how I hit it or how they hit it. I was really just trying to beat them. But you have to remember it was very different on tour then. We didn't get free balls on tour until 1986. John Mahaffey would change the lie angle of his clubs on the curb. There were no equipment trucks. I would actually wait until I got home to change grips. The Tommy Armour irons I played in '86, the sweet spot would hold water. The center of the clubs were literally concaved and would hold water."

Gallagher would lose his PGA Tour card during the '87 campaign. During the five-year run he had won on two professional tournaments, not PGA Tour events, but they were still wins. He had played with many of the best players in the game and had grown as a player and person. The grind of battling for position on the PGA Tour was getting to Jim after that '87 season.

"The toll of the PGA Tour was beginning to take hold of me. It was like one day was perfect and the next day was just horrible. My mood, to some degree, was based around what I had shot that day and for good reason as I needed to shoot good numbers to keep my job. I remember times during the '87 season that I just wanted the year to end. But that only meant that I would have to go back to tour school again

"I was a very blue-collar kid that happened to have a dad who work at a country club. I knew how to work hard and that didn't bother me. I was twenty-six years old and can still remember thinking 'What am I going to do if I don't play golf?' For as long as I can remember that is what I had worked hard at doing. All my energy was put into being a better and better player. Of course, I had a marketing degree from Tennessee but that was years away from being a profession.

"I had put my whole life into trying to play professional golf. I didn't go out drinking or partying in high school or college. I gave up a lot of social stuff because playing golf was my dream and I wasn't going to let anything get in my way. My dream was there, I was playing golf on the PGA Tour. The dream is there and I am in it. Eighty-seven was so hard because I had tasted it.

Jim Gallagher Jr. had played in 113 PGA Tour events when he lost his PGA Tour Card for the '88 season. Jimmy and some of his friends were thinking about playing in South Africa or possibly just on mini tours. Jim decided to play a few mini tour events and Monday qualify for tour events.

Jim Monday qualified for **eight** events in 1988. Monday qualifying for a PGA Tour event is difficult, very difficult. On the Monday before every PGA Tour event (with exception to Invitationals and Majors) there is a tournament held. The field of players can range from forty to one hundred fifty players and they are playing for only four spots. It is a shoot-out of sorts with only eighteen holes to decide who will get in the event and when a player gets into the field in this manner, they are generally referred to as Monday Qualifiers.

"Then I finished second in Milwaukee." Jim begins. Understand that a second- place finish after Monday Qualifying into a PGA Tour Event rarely, if ever, happens. A second-place finish earned Jim a better eligibility ranking, and he would get in more events through the rest of the summer and into the fall. Milwaukee was in September of '88 and in November of that same year Jim would be playing in the Centel Classic and would need to finish in the top 40 to keep his card.

"The last day I birdied 17 and almost made birdie on 18. I knew I was close but when I got to the scoreboard, I couldn't count past five because my head was spinning. My buddy Denny Hepler was there telling me, 'You are in! You made it! You are in,' but I just couldn't count. It was like I was in shock. I can remember driving to the airport and still not believing I was in.

"At the airport I saw a PGA Tour official and I just strode up to him and asked if I had made it. 'Jimmy, congratulations you officially finished 124th on the money list and have your PGA Tour Card for the next year.' That was when I finally believed it. I had lived out of my car nearly the entire year and had gone through all those Monday qualifiers.

But there was something else that happened in 1988. Jim Jr. had a change in mindset. He had met a family just before Easter of that year. "I guess I grew up. All I know is my perspective changed. I realized that golf shouldn't dictate my personality. I realized that golf wasn't my whole life."

The first final stage I personally coached was at PGA West in the California desert. It was the first year of the new rule change by the PGA Tour. Beginning in 1962, PGA Tour Qualifying School was the way to get a PGA Tour Card. In 2012 Tim Finchem, PGA Tour commissioner, and the PGA Tour Policy board made a fifty-year change to Q- School. So in 2013 the Web.com Tour became the way to get a PGA Tour Card, and instead of being the PGA Tour Qualifying School it became the Web.com Tour Qualifying School.

In 2013 Matt Fast, Jonathan Randolph, Matt Hughes, Will Strickler and Carlos Sainz were the kids that Tim Yelverton (short game guru) had at the finals. As coaches we kept our boys on task and hungry for pushing themselves by encouraging them to focus on what they could control. There was a whole lot they couldn't control.

The PGA Tour was giving the top forty-nine players status on the Web.com Tour. First place would receive a fully exempt status, 2nd through 10th, 12 exemptions, 11th through, 49th, 8 exemptions, 50th or less would result in status on the Tour but very little chance of getting in an event. Looking through the lens of the player it is easy to see why players refer to Tour School as one of the toughest weeks of performance mentally and physically.

That year three players gained status on the Web.com Tour. Carlos Sainz earned twelve starts. Jonathan Randolph and Matt Fast both earned eight starts. Matt Hughes and Will Strickler obtained status on the Web.com Tour but did not get any starts in the 2014 season.

ONLY ONE SHOT

7

¿HABLAS EL IDIOMA DE LOS CAMPEONES?

How should I speak to my children? Should I praise them for their accomplishments or for their work ethic? Do I want my junior golfer to love learning or love winning? The Language of Champions introduces some key terms: Fixed Mindset and Growth Mindset and provides a new understanding of **How Important Your Words Are To Your Junior Golfer.**

How many times have you heard the phrase: "It is not what you say, but how you say it."? Coaching hour after hour, I know and understand the complicated game of golf. I genuinely understand that it is not what I say, it is how I say it. One of the most difficult aspects of conveying a message is putting your message in the right terms for your intended audience. It takes time to learn this skill. As a parent, it is worth your time to hone this skill.

I have been around people who are very good at this game and people who are very bad at this game. I have been around hard-headed people who were really good at golf and hard-headed people who were quite bad. The same is true for open- minded and closed-minded people. There is not a perfect brain among great players, and they have many different personality characteristics. To communicate with great players, you need to speak their language

An Interpretation of Hogan's Quote

What is the language of champions? What makes them hear differently from the rest of the players? Why is it that some kids get extremely angry on the driving range and some do not? Why do some excel and others do not?

> "My family wasn't rich, they were poor. I feel sorry for rich kids now, I really do. Because they are never going to have the opportunity I had. Because I knew tough things and I had a tough day all my life. And I can handle tough things, they can't. And every day that I progressed was a joy to me. And I recognized it every day."

--Ben Hogan

Mr. Hogan's point wasn't about being rich or poor. After all, at the time of this interview he was very wealthy. He spent his adult life at the best golf clubs in the world. His friends were mostly prominent businessmen. Mr. Hogan also understood that money was vital to getting chances. A successful businessman named Marvin Leonard played a key role in his development. I am sure he had seen successful kids on both sides of the fence. This is my interpretation of Mr. Hogan's quote:

> *"My family wasn't something special. I feel sorry for kids who come from families that have been really successful because they are never going to have the opportunity to learn the way I did. My family knew how tough things could be and nearly every day for my family was hard. I can handle tough days because I know I can learn from them. Every day I was thankful that I got to learn something. I don't have to live up to someone else's standard for me.*

The further I travel down the road as a golf instructor, the more I see one clear difference. **Children who enjoy learning do much better than children who enjoy being good at the game**. You can see the boundaries that sometimes go up around adolescents. They expect the good shots, are annoyed by average shots and have difficulty receiving instruction. Many times, this same child was extremely hungry for knowledge only years before. What could have happened?

The fifty or so high school state champions I have instructed, are predominantly from middle-class families. Do wealthy parents give their children everything while middle-class families make their children work for it? My experience working with people from all socio-economic backgrounds does not point to this conclusion. Having monetary means only helps the child do more, but there does seem to be a tipping point.

Do you really want to be great? How would it feel to be the world's best golfer? Remember, once you are number one there is nowhere to go except down. That is part of the intrigue with Tom Brady, Tiger Woods, Jack Nicklaus or Michael Jordan. They did not seem to be bothered by being number one.

Dr. Carol Dweck, a Stanford University psychologist, has researched many questions about a child's aptitude for learning. She defines two types of people: Fixed Minded and Growth Minded. Her premise is simple: Fixed-Minded people will avoid being shown up by opportunities to learn; Growth-Minded people will steer INTO learning opportunities. Everyone exhibits instances of being Fixed- Minded and Growth-Minded.

My first recollection of being Fixed-Minded was with my father. He loved motorcycles. A full day riding motorcycles through trails couldn't be topped for him. While a sense of adventure did appeal to me when I was young, I really did not truly enjoy riding motorcycles. But a boy will follow his father, and I rode.

The message my father sent was very clear. Talking to my mother, he said, "VJ's got it. He handled that bike like a veteran today." I was probably nine or ten-years- old at the time, and I completely understood the situation. My father had just said I was good at riding a bike; I had accomplished my mission. My father was proud of me because I had proved I could cruise the trails. Mission accomplished

I was now labeled as a veteran. I didn't want to prove my father wrong, so I had nowhere to go but down. At first, I felt a bit nervous riding the bike after that. He probably noticed my reluctance and started handing out advice. The advice was given kindly at first. Then it became more dynamic. I developed the "yips" when it came to riding motorcycles! All this transpired over about a six-month period. One day, it seemed he gave up on me riding bikes. What a great day for me—I was absolutely thrilled!

He praised me for my ability. I was convinced I was really good at riding a motorcycle. Then, I began to second-guess myself because I didn't want to make an error that would prove him (or me) wrong. I made errors and then I got advice. But I didn't think I needed the advice (outcome-oriented thinking). I thought I was letting us both down. I had completely fallen from grace. How was that possible? Now I just wanted out.

So, what went wrong? I was praised and embodied that praise for being "a veteran" when, in truth, I was really just a beginner. If I had heard my father say, "Your son really gave it a lot of effort today. He has a lot to learn, but I think he enjoys it," then I would have probably looked at motorcycling much differently.

I have made the same mistakes as a father, too. On the 12th hole of our home course, on July 4th, 2009, my seven-year-old son made a hole-in-one from the women's tee. He took out his little blue driver, hopped on the tee, swung and made it. It was unreal. People all around the club talked about it, saying things like, "I didn't have my first one until I was 40!" or "I have never made one!" What did I say to my son? "You are different. You are going to make more hole-in-ones than them." Oops!

Dr. Carol Dweck: Praise Effort

Dr. Carol Dweck has argued over and over again that praising our children for effort is better than praising them for an innate quality. When our children are praised for effort, they are in control. They can be resilient, have time to grow, learn and understand. When we praise our children for being the best or for being winners, we are praising an outcome. Our children are not in control of outcomes. Their time for growth, learning or understanding is diminished **because they must now win as they learn.**

You want to hear one of the greatest ways to mess up a fellow golfer? As they are looking over a putt, casually say, **"You haven't missed a putt that short in years."** The Fixed-Minded person who resides in all of us immediately feels some emotion or begins to hear some voices, sending your brain a clear message: "You are a great putter. If you miss this one, well, your streak will be broken." What generally happens next?

Telling your children they are the best might sound like a helpful way to grow their confidence, but such words really work in the opposite way. Such high praise can set up a situation where your child will actually go out of their way to be the best. This means they can miss a critical step in the evolution of becoming great, which is learning to lose. It can lead to them being envious of other players' successes. It can lead to a child who sees instruction as criticism. It can lead them to become defensive when the going gets tough. Eventually, it can lead to them giving up on the game.

Why do parents tell their children they are special, that they are the best? Why do parents praise accomplishments? The focus of your praise should be on learning, not on accomplishing

Telling your children that you are proud of them for having the will to learn might not seem fruitful in the beginning, yet it could be the cornerstone to create confidence and set up situations where they will actually seek to be tested. This search means your child will learn that being beaten in a competition is part of the learning process and they will also learn from the success of other players. The child begins to see instruction as an opportunity to learn more. Finally, such a focus means your child will embrace being challenged when the going gets tough.

Young junior players with a fixed mindset do not see effort as a desirable quality. They think, "Effort is for those who were not born great." I see this mindset quite often in our teaching center. These children believe they were born with an innate quality that places them above and beyond their competition. Effort, to them, is for other people. "He gets it really quick!" would be the parent's comment even before the child actually "gets it." You must understand that anyone who learns anything quickly understands the process of how to learn. A PGA Tour player might "learn" something quickly, but rarely, if ever, will a young junior golfer learn quickly when they are building motor skills.

Because the fixed-mindset junior player believes effort is for other players, they often fight taking control of the process. The word "process" implies effort. If there is no process, there is no plan. If there is no plan, there is no deliberate effort. The lack of a process is the most disabling aspect of the fixed mind in junior golf. If your junior golfer will not get involved in the process, they are asking to be devoured by the outcome.

In the end, the fixed-mindset junior player finds success with only winning or accomplishing external goals. In golf this is a dead-end street. Even the most elite golfers win only a small percentage of the time as they go from the different learning and competitive phases. An early start in golf can lead to multiple wins when everyone else is learning to play. But as your young junior leaves their small pond, they will find many other golfers who are equally skilled.

Young junior players with a growth mindset see effort as a desirable quality. They see that pushing themselves daily changes the way they eventually putt or swing. They see the ball fly better or roll well as a by-product of their effort. I do my best to teach this mindset in my shop. Effort to them is what will create their successes. The reason you don't see PGA Tour players standing on the range for five hours is because they are practicing by objectives, not time. Remind your growth mindset juniors that your desire is that they practice with an objective. Set the objective in practice, accomplish it, and then go play.

Because the growth-mindset junior views effort as a desirable quality, they get involved in the process. The process in golf is mental, strategic, physical, technical and nutritional. Often times you will see some of the best juniors rearranging their bags, cleaning their clubs, marking their ball a certain way, etc. It looks a bit "OCD" or at least "superstitious," but the reality is these activities are simply an offshoot of the process. At elite levels, the process means more than the win because the win is a by-product of the process.

In the end, the growth-mindset junior finds success with objective effort and accomplishing internal goals. I whole-heartedly believe this is what Mr. Hogan is saying in his quote. The process becomes the primary focus. The art of learning is self-taught via a process that makes growth the true goal.

So how do we create a child with lofty goals while living in a nurturing environment? The first thing I always do is listen. I listen to children. I listen to their body language, to their words, to their eyes and to their actions. Becoming a good listener takes many, many hours of deliberate practice. Begin by reminding your children you are proud of their daily effort. Remind them that you will let them go to tournaments or take lessons only if they put in the "behind the scenes" effort needed to work on their objectives. If I can get a child and parent to be accountable off the course to do their deliberate practice, we are on the right track.

The Golf Course

Let's look at being on the golf course where things get a little tricky. It is true that score is all that matters on the course. You simply must instill the belief that score is a by-product of a good process. Make the routine the primary objective. Let them know that sometimes the conditions might be set against them. They might not shoot the lowest number of their life on a given day, but they will have the opportunity to practice their routines each time out. They will have the chance, hole after hole, to laugh at the emotions and go through their routines. They will have the chance to learn how a ball comes out of wet Bermuda grass. Every day on the course can either be an exhibition of emotional hijacking or an opportunity to place trust in their routine and the deliberate practice underlying the routine.

You should cultivate the notion that the golf course is also a **great place to learn about golf.** Avoid thinking that the course is only a place to score or win tournaments. Teach your children, through words and actions, that the golf course is a place where they can experience the sport and learn many things needed to grow as a player. Stay away from the mindset that a course is only a place to judge their understanding of the sport. Tournaments are the judge of how well a golfer understands the game. My thinking is that the golf course is a place for growth: mental, emotional, strategic and mechanical.

As you and your child build a growth mindset together, you must be aware of how to "layer the process" with specific physical activities that enhance your child's golf swing and body. You layer the process with a more defined routine and with deliberation in their practice. Just layer and layer and while not judging their talent. Instead, judge, reward and encourage their growth in the process. Applaud them for their daily practice. Applaud them for playing six holes running their routines. Applaud them for nearly any effort that has an objective.

You are most likely looking for a disciplined, but loving, environment for your child to learn about golf. This overnight. Moreover, it will never appear if you place external achievements above internal growth. Keep it simple. Expect full participation, mentally and physically, in a developmentally appropriate process.

My father always goes back to my boxing days. Over the course of writing this book, we discussed many things. He says time-and-time again that when I was boxing, I went from a mediocre soccer player to a "coach's first choice." I went from an average tennis player to "a player with some aggression." I went from a little guy swinging a club to "a club champion."

Whether the mental toughness of facing someone in the ring changed me or whether the stimulus of movement hit my growth velocity at the right time will be debatable between us for some time. To me, this is what really happened. I started believing that I could get better at something that I never thought I could tackle. The more I hit that bag, the easier it was to perform in the ring. I took control of a process for the first time and my life changed.

It will be difficult to watch your children fail. I'm like you. It is not fun for me so see my children in tears. It is not easy for me to explain to my children they are not the best in the world. Parenting is simply not for cowards. Be courageous and think differently. Tell your children that failing just means their process needs to be tighten up a little bit. Tell them they are expected to give full effort in the preparation for a tournament. Give them the courage to let the tournament decide the winner. If you are going to speak the language of champions, you must learn it. Go ahead, be courageous and LEARN!

In closing I want to address one more observation I have made over the years. "Well Johnny just likes team sports. He likes being a part of a team." Hogwash! Every child wants to be special, really special. They dream of it! Team sports, however, are a great place for a child with a fixed mindset to hide. Just go ask coaches of team sports and they will tell you how difficult it is to keep the team competing as a unit. One of their biggest tasks is to keep the super-stars simply doing their own job on the field.

If a child is not using all their potential or is having a bad day, golf is the worst sport in the world to play. As parents, you will probably hear this sentiment. Over the years, there will be times when football or softball will pop up for no apparent reason. There is absolutely nothing wrong with team sports. After all, you and I are a part of a team every day at work. Just try to examine the situation and make certain that your child's mindset is not driving the desire to play team sports. You must work to extinguish the fixed mindset in your child. You must be prepared to do so many, many times.

Chapter Lessons:

- **Children who enjoy learning do much better in golf than children who enjoy winning.**

- Think about what it is that draws your compliments toward your children.

- Be courageous: watch your children fail and teach them to focus on the process.

- Fixed mindsets are created quickly. You must extinguish them quicker.

8

HUH?

Some stories are worth telling. In a small southern town, there were two players, a U.S. KIDS World Champion and a USGA Championship Semi-Finalist. Such honors seem unlikely at first glance. According to a recent census, the population of the town is 4,032—1,835 females and 2,197 males. The estimated medium household income is $25,294. There is one golf course—with only nine holes. The name of the town is Fulton, Mississippi.

The story begins with the birth of Chad Ramey, the only son of Stanley and Trish Ramey. Their home was nearly on a golf course like the homes of many club professionals in the rural south. At the age of three, Chad began swinging a golf club. Whether it was from his close proximity to the course or his awareness of people swinging clubs all around him, Stanley thought Chad "looked like a player when he started swinging." The young man's contact was good at age three. By the age of seven, he started getting serious about golf. In his first tournament, a recognized regional event, he finished 5th with only five clubs in the bag. Chad won his second tournament: The Pepsi Little People's, played in Illinois.

Close by, Jamie McDonald was charged most afternoons with entertaining his three-year-old daughter, Ally, because his wife, Angie, worked an odd shift. Because he was a golfer, Jaime decided he would cut down a club (either a 3- or 7-iron) as a toy for Ally. She immensely enjoyed hitting the little plastic balls in the backyard. She had so much fun that Jaime began to take her to the golf course with him when she was a five-year-old.

Jaime had this to say, "After seeing her for a while at the course, Stanley told me she had some talent." The seemingly "talented" little girl had honed her skills with the plastic balls in the backyard using her father's cut-down iron.

By age nine, Chad had accomplished an extraordinary feat: he won the U.S. KIDS World Championship. The tournament is likely the largest junior golf tournament in the world, hosting a field of over twelve hundred players from thirty countries.

Both children grew up playing multiple sports. Chad played t-ball, baseball, golf and a little junior high football. Ally grew up with softball, basketball and golf. She would come home from a weekend of softball tournaments and play in a golf tournament the next day. "I hate softball," her father remembers her saying.

Chad, on the other hand, decided reasonably early that golf was a better sport for him. "He told me at about seven-years-old that if I would take him to golf tournaments, he would back away from baseball," Stanley recalls. While Ally continued to play basketball competitively throughout high school, Chad chose golf as his only competitive outlet. He played other sports, but more for fun than competitively. With the golf course in the backyard, he felt that golf was really just a way of life.

After three years of competition Chad had racked up thirty-one wins in tournament play. The start for the young Ally wasn't quite as glorious. As her father recalls, "At about age twelve, she played in The Pepsi Little People's—her first regional event. She was disqualified for a rules violation. It wasn't anything intentional; it involved a breach of the rules with a lost ball. Our whole family was there, ever her grandparents. We were all disappointed, but it was what it was."

One of the advantages she had, however, was the chance to follow the path of the slightly older Chad Ramey. Jaime recounts, "We went from playing the course, to playing a local tour, to playing the state's junior circuit. Being the only girl around in her age group was also an advantage. Nearly each time out, all the other competitors were boys. Also, the more she played in tournaments, the more she liked it."

My questions, of course, were "What laid behind the scenes? How much did they practice and play?" Stanley Ramey replied, "We would do something five or six days a week. It might not be much, but it would be something. Gradually, using their attention span as a guide, we would practice more. In his younger years, it was just the two of us. Ally had not joined us. When Chad was young, we might just play four holes. Later on, if he could keep his attention, we might play be nine holes. We did a lot of drills in the house, too. I would say maybe fifteen or twenty minutes, three or four days a week."

"For Ally," recalls the Jaime, "there was always a good bit of practice. Early on it was just fun. As she got older, she might spend about two hours a week working on her mechanics. Early on, of course, there was some ball pounding on the range. But as she got older, she became more deliberate about her practice. When her coach began to change her swing, there was a lot of mirror practice at home. To tell the truth, doing the drills was like pulling teeth. She hated having her score suffer on the golf course—so that helped her embrace the drills."

Looking back, the players recall it a bit differently. "I never really beat balls five or six hours a day," Ally recalls. "I guess it has always been more quality than quantity. My dad helped me practice correctly. Sometimes I have to think of things differently and he would always be out there helping me

"I did most of my drills at home and then I would go to the golf course. One year I had a bunch of drills marked down for the things I needed to do with my swing."

So how would two kids, one who had to be coached via his attention span and the other to whom "doing drills was like pulling teeth," grow into two young adults who talk about quality versus quantity and embrace the idea of drills?

"They were both so different," recalls Stanley. "Ally could stay out there all day long, but Chad could not. Practice for both of them was always as intentional and deliberate as I could make it. They were always working on their swings; the ball flight or the score was not the instructor. I would sit back and watch, and I knew what they needed to do with their swings and the both received instruction and feedback well. They bought into the process of building good motion. They trusted what their swing instructor and I were saying and learned not to take short cuts."

"In the past four years," recalls Ally's father, Jaime, "she has become more and more deliberate in her practice. She played so many rounds and nearly all of them had a purpose. Her goal was pretty clear by age twelve: play college golf and play on the LPGA Tour after that. We reminded her that reaching these goals meant she would miss out on some things other children would be doing."

Stanley understood the process of building good motion. The process of standing in front of the mirror working on their motions was something they could control. Standing on the range making good swings was something they could control. "We always tried to use drills. As we progressed, eventually we would look at ball flight," recalls Chad. "I never really worried about ball flight until I got close to a tournament." Ally says it like this, "Get your feel from drills. It is very important to know how the correct motion should feel before hitting a golf ball."

Both sets of parents created the template for success. They graded their children by how well they worked and how much they worked. Stanley tried to teach both children only when they were capable of listening, and he used their attention spans as a guideline.

For parents who are constantly grading their children by their golf scores and ball flight, listen to the answers to the following question: "If you wanted to make a really bad junior golfer, what would you tell them?"

Chad's answer "I would tell them to worry about ball flight. The thing my Dad and I have always said is that we get our feel from mechanics instead of ball flight. I would also tell them to play all the time while worrying about the ball flight and trying to hit it correctly."

Ally's answer: "I would say practice all the time worrying about ball flight. The junior player will get tired practicing all day and they will get frustrated from the ball flight not being correct. I would also tell them to get the feel of their swing from ball flight."

My next question "If you wanted to make a great junior golfer what would you tell them?" Chad's answer: "I would tell them to go out and play. Learn to get the ball around the course—no matter how good or bad. Then, I would tell them to get their feels from drills. Go in a progression with the swing." Ally: "I would say play golf, but still do drills. Play, practice, and do drills in equal amounts. Practice, for me, is when I hit a golf ball. Drills are when there is no ball and I am concentrating on how I am moving. The drills make the practice and the practice makes the playing."

Knowing what to do but not doing it enough is really useless. My next question to them both was a simple one: "Have you practiced 10,000 hours?" Chad replied: "Yes. I would say so. I miss a few days, but I try not to. I try to do something every day. I haven't missed too many days." Ally added: "I would probably be pretty close. It may not be over 10,000 hours. I never have thought that I had been out there that much. But when you throw the numbers at me, I guess I have."

These two children grew up listening to a golf course manager who preached effort and doing your best. They were taught to practice and work on the things they could control instead of things that they could not. Both sets of parents created a culture of hard, steady work. Both children devoted countless hours working on perfecting the process of learning.

Their combined results:

- 4 individual State High School Championships
- 3 High School State Team Championships
- 5 State Junior Championships

- 1 US Kids World Championship
- 8 Exxon/BFI Championships
- 2 Pepsi Little People's Championships
- 1 Women's State Amateur Championship
- 1 Trusted Choice Big "I" National Championship
- 1 USGA Semi-finalist
- 2014 Curtis Cup Member
- 2017 Canadian Tour Member
- 2016 Symetra Tour 2nd Place on Money List
- 2017 LPGA Tour Rookie
- 2018 Web.com Tour Rookie
- 2018 LPGA Tour Member

But the question still lingers: "Why?" Why did this all happen in such a short span and in such a small town?

"It was Stanley Ramey," says Jaime McDonald. "He saw something in my daughter and said so repeatedly. He convinced us to have her start playing in competition. Stanley remarked, "I had confidence in the kids, in the swing instructor, and I enjoyed watching them get better and I knew they could get even better! They outworked ninety percent of the others but worked with intent. To me, it was just being honest with the kids, being truthful—good or bad. Once they realize you are just being honest with them it gets easier."

When the players were asked why they chose golf, Chad said, "I love golf, it is my lifestyle. I like going to different places and competing with everyone." Ally answered, "I have had a goal for years. I know the highest-level players work hard. I might not be the most talented, but I know if I work hard, I can get there. There have been some sacrifices. Stanley, my swing instructor, and the people around me were all telling me that I could be great. It helps to know that people see your potential."

It is easy to see how the hard work came together. As the children matured, their attention spans governed the teaching time. As they learned, the emphasis was put on them, not the ball flight or score. Both kids said their parents never reprimanded them for a physical error on the course. Only mental errors were pointed out—because the players had control over their decisions. They were not worried about ball flight during practice sessions. They were focused on moving correctly. Both players were raised in a culture that praised effort and approaching the game correctly—results were simply results. Both of them put in thousands of hours of intentional practice. When asked what they were thinking about when they played, both of them said, "Our routines, mostly. We always use playing to work on our routines."

But something else happened. The golf club got involved. The older men at the club followed the kids' exploits. Their pictures adorned the walls of the pro shop. Kids from neighboring towns began to win big events around the state. It seems that not only did the children learn a great process, but they also gave other kids the belief they could do it too.

I asked them all, "Do you think what was accomplished by these two players will ever happen again?" All four respondents began the answer with deep sighs. One commented "Whooooo! I don't think so, not in the near future." Another said, "I hope so, but it will be hard." Still another said, "No. I really don't see anybody at our age doing what we did."

But I think the Ally summed it up the best. "I want to say there is a possibility, but I don't know. With the people I see around Fulton Country Club, golf is not really a sport anyone is interested in. There are kids that come out, but they are not really serious. I don't really know why we pursued golf the way we did. I guess just because.... I don't really know why it happened. I guess you could say God put us here and that was it."

The name of this chapter, "HUH?" comes from what most people say when they learn the identity of the town where these two are from. "Huh? Now, where is that?" would be the common back. The moral of this story is simple. Facilities and equipment do not build champions. People build champions.

Even though the moral of the story generally is the last part of a story, I want to add some additional quotes from the interviews as an epilogue. I hope you enjoy them as much as I did.

What are the biggest stumbling blocks for parents?

"There is a line. You can't be too nice, but you can't stay constantly pissed at them either. The worst I have seen is on the course is when the parents get mad at their children."

"I know they want their kids to do really well, but they push them too hard in performance. My dad pushed me to practice, not really to perform. With playing, he never got on to me for what I physically did wrong. He always reflected on what I was thinking about when I hit the shot. When I would get lazy, he would remind me to do my drills. It was never really the performance side."

When did golf become instinctive?

"Wow. I really don't know. She really loved golf from the beginning. Really, she was gifted early to a point where she would relax and play. At about age fourteen, she thought she was supposed to win. I would say that little girl in the back yard hitting balls was doing it instinctively. How do you explain that? My explanation is that it is God given."

"I don't know if it is completely instinctive now. They are still learning. They had a little bit of golfing talent, but they worked so hard. When we go back and look at their swings at age eight or ten compared to the swings now, it isn't even close. When they were growing up, people would say to me, 'Why do you want to take him to a golf guru and screw up his swing?' They just didn't understand."

What do you think is the most important factor in creating these two golfers?

"I think so much of it was him playing in the junior events really young and having success. Chad won the US Kids by age ten or so. He had things going for him early that made him believe he could really play with anybody When Ally started, she had mentors. As an eighth grader, she and the other girls on the high school team won their first time out. I don't think she really knew how good she was until she made it to the US Junior Semis."

"Fundamentals. The fundamentals of playing, of their mechanic, and of their minds grew together. It wasn't ball flight or scores. It was more the process of integrating fundamentals. I say process, process and process all the time to them. They do a wonderful job of staying in the present—staying in the present begins with practice. In 2007, they won their first state championship. A guy was there giving away a book, Golf's Sacred Journey: Seven Days at the Links of Utopia. *We used a lot of information from the book,* **Focus on the present. All we can control is what we are doing right now. Don't get ahead of yourself, and don't look back."**

What would be your normal day in the summer?

"Get up at 7:30 or 8:00. Go out and hit balls for an hour, putt and chip.

Take a break, go play nine holes. Take a break. Work around the greens some more, be at the course all day but not practice all day. Mentally, I can't go full bore from sunrise to sunset. I know what I am going to work on every day before I go out. When I am on the golf course, I always go through my routine. No matter what is happening on the course, I am repeatedly going through my routine ."

"Get up around 8:30, be at the course by 10:00. I would drill and practice for a couple of hours. Then lunch. Get loose and then go play nine or eighteen holes. Normally after I play, I focus on what I didn't do well, and I would go work on it for one hour or so. A day would last from 10:00 till 6:00 or so."

- Based on an interview in 2012 – Recent additions to collective achievements added in Winter of 2017

9

The Rise

Greenwood, Mississippi, was a booming town in the mid 1900s, just like most of the Mississippi Delta. The crop that was making it all happen was cotton. With the business of cotton booming the game of golf began to grow.

Ed Meeks and Linda Dycus grew up in this same hometown. Ed finished college at Mississippi State University in Agriculture Economics. Linda went to Blue Mountain College on a voice scholarship and transferred to Mississippi University for Women. They got married and had three children, Keasler Meeks born in 1964, Cissye Meeks born in 1966 and Beth Meeks born in 1967. During that time Ed became a very good golfer. He was self-taught, loved the competition and had won the Mississippi State Amateur.

"I played a lot of golf when I was a kid," Cissye said. "I am sure I went to every State Amateur with my dad beginning in 1974. I was a little girl but he always took me. My brother liked to hunt and be on the farm, so it just made sense for him to take me.

"When I was thirteen, I showed up for the State Junior and my dad and I talked the tournament staff into letting me play in the fifteen to nineteen-year-old age group. I won and qualified for USGA Girls in Colorado. Heather and Missy Farr were next door in our hotel. Heather was the number one ranked player in the country at that time and twenty-four hours after meeting them and their parents, we were having dinner together.

"At the time we didn't know Heather was the best junior in the country. It was a new world to me. I was fourteen and this was the first tournament I had ever played where it was all girls!

"Heather and her family really introduced us to the AJGA. Because of my play in Mississippi and Louisiana, I got in all the AJGA events I wanted. When I was sixteen Buddy Alexander, the coach at Louisiana State University, started watching me play. I would eventually sign a scholarship with LSU and play college golf for Buddy. "

Cissye played at LSU from 1984 to 1989 and met Jim through a team-mate. Jackie Gallagher, Jim's sister, and Cissye met at the USGA Girl's Junior in Seattle, Washington. "It just so happened that Jackie and I stayed in guest housing at that event with families that were best friends. Jackie and I became friends and stayed in touch as pen pals.

"We would see each other at more tournaments throughout the summer and I think she was getting recruited by a bunch of schools. At Onion Creek Golf Club at the Future Legends she ruptured her Achilles tendon. She had surgery and all the recruiting stopped.

"With a boot on her injured leg she won the Indiana State Girls Championship. I told Buddy Alexander and he brought her to LSU where she would go on to be an All-American and play the LPGA Tour.

"In '88 she mentioned that her brother Jim Gallagher was playing in a professional event in Jackson, Mississippi. I was visiting my mother, who at the time was being treated for cancer in the hospital there. She was diagnosed in my freshman year in high school and had been fighting cancer for seven years.

"On our very first date Jim met my mom. He finished the tournament and we were going to dinner. We had met before when Jim came to an event or two to watch his sister Jackie play. Jim came to the hospital room to pick me up. Soon after that, I invited my whole team to my home in Greenwood for Easter weekend. My mom wanted everyone to come so Jim got the invite too.

"That was the first weekend he got to spend with my mom, and it was the first time Jim got to see our family dynamic up close and personal." Cissye recalled. What Cissye may have not known at that time was how much the Meeks family was affecting him. In that house, with Cissye's mom battling cancer, with her father working to pay the medical bills, Jim found a very positive family filled with faith and that encounter changed his mindset.

"If I played badly it didn't mean I was a bad person and if I played well it didn't mean that I was a great person. I didn't have a sports psychologist, I thought if I discussed what was going on in my mind it was a weakness. I think a lot of us as players thought that. But being on the PGA Tour every week can change your life and things add up quickly.

"But when Linda Meeks is facing chemo treatment and asking me about my family and who I really was, it moved me. I knew the 'Jim Gallagher pity party' had to end. On tour it is so easy to sit around and grumble and find others to do the same. Linda had every reason to complain but she wasn't. She was living. She was fighting. She opened my eyes and after meeting her I approached the game completely differently.

"In '85, '86 and '87 I was approaching things wrong. When I met Cissye I found a young lady who had her world turned upside down, family and the game of golf. So, it didn't take too much reflection to see that my mindset was just awful. I was playing the best tour in the world and I had somehow made that a bad thing."

In 1989 Jimmy's life took a turn for the better. "I had a purpose driven life by then." Jimmy's finish on the money list in the 1988 season had given him what players on the PGA Tour desire, a defined schedule, to add to that new mindset. On the PGA Tour there are a dozen or players each week who are playing to stabilize their schedules. For the high priority ranked players, they can plan vacations with their families or simply take time to relax and get away from the game. They can even plan time for some technique adjustments. It is stability and for a traveling professional stability can mean a lot.

But there was another stable factor now in Jimmy's life. As the 1989 year-end money list proves Jim Gallagher was a different player. In the wake of the hair- raising year of 1988, he won over a quarter of a million dollars on the PGA Tour. His next best year up to that point was $83,766. That stable factor was the girl from the Mississippi Delta, Cissye Gallagher.

Cissye's influence on Jim was almost immediate. Around here we often say, "emotion builds motion." Jim comments in a similar way when recalling how meeting Linda Meeks changed his "mindset." In many cases we want more than that to explain accomplishments. We want there to be some change in technique or some change in equipment or even a change in philosophy. But the truth is that each of us are influenced by those around us, and we in turn influence those we are around.

Jim and Cissye had a busy '89 and '90. They wed in November of 1989 and Cissye went to tour school and got her conditional card for the LPGA Tour. After a career best year on the PGA Tour Jim began following the tour.

"Cissye actually spent our honeymoon with me at the mixed team. In fact, she actually caddied for me during our honeymoon! What the hell were we thinking! Anyway, that is how we started our marriage. The first six months of the year we were on opposites sides of the country. She was playing the LPGA Tour and I was playing the PGA Tour. We were both living our dreams. "

By July of Cissye's rookie year an old injury re-surfaced. "I remember she told me in July or so of 1990 that she could barely even lift her arm above her head. She was debating what to do with her life. She wanted kids and a family just as I did, but she also was a rookie on the LPGA Tour, a goal she had spent countless hours in pursuit of since she was a child.

"I wanted her to do what she wanted, of course, but I didn't want her to give up her career. I wanted her to keep playing because it was her dream too. Then I won Milwaukee." In dramatic fashion Jimmy won in a playoff against Ed Dougherty and Billy Mayfair. On the 17th hole, which was the first playoff hole, Jimmy bested the field and was officially a tour winner.

"I am now a tour winner! I am off the charts excited. We had a long talk, and Cissye decided to have shoulder surgery and become a mother. At the end of '90 Cissye gave up her dream in the world of golf.

"She decided she could not be the kind of wife and mother she wanted to be if she kept playing."

I was growing up. Cissye gave up her dream and career so that I could pursue mine. I hate to say it, but I would have never made that decision at that point in my life. I watched someone who had worked as hard as I did, for all those years, look into her future and make a decision to move on. Once again, the reality of being an evolved human versus the reality of winning on tour hit me in the face again."

Jimmy's technique and body had remained basically the same through all those years. His equipment, eating habits, shoes and clothing were the same. There was no sports psychologist. What changed was his mindset about the game; Cissye inspired Jimmy.

Jim's 1st Masters

"I gotta rock and roll. Here is the beauty of winning. I am in The Masters and exempt to all the big tournaments. In the fall of '90 I know where my schedule is going to take us. We buy a house in Greenwood. I was learning to get away from the game some. I was learning to hunt, be a husband, to be a home-owner and Ed and Linda Meeks' son-in-law. The more I learned to get away from the game the better I played. The day I met Linda in March of 1988, my whole world off the course changed. "On the course I was just seeing shots and hitting them. There was no swing change or technique I was working toward. I was just playing golf. Then April rolled around, and it was time for the Masters. I will never forget the beginning of the week because the PGA Tour wanted to mic me and video tape my practice round.

My first practice round was with Phil Mickelson and Ian Baker-Finch and a film crew for the entire practice round. Mickelson was an amateur and they are filming me the entire practice round. So, my first time at Augusta is with a film crew, Phil and Ian. Second practice round was with Freddy (Couples) and Tim Simpson.

"I remember going out that first day and getting on the first tee and really not knowing if I was going to make contact. I was so nervous. On the first hole, I pulled it in the trees. I got it up and down at 17. Made par at 18. But I had a goal. I wanted to get some crystal. 'Get some crystal Jimmy,' I remember saying to myself. I shot 67 and was leading.

"Best part was Ed (Cissye's dad) calling me, probably from a bag phone in his truck. He and Linda were on the way over.

"So, Jimmy how did you do?" I remember him asking.

"Good I responded. I shot 67 and I'm in the lead. In the background I hear Linda's voice saying, 'Ed I told you I heard that he was leading on the radio. I told you!'

"But Ed and Linda didn't believe it until they got there. It was really pretty special. My mom and dad, Cissye's mom and dad, my brother and sister and the president of Tommy Armour Golf all got to experience that with me. It was cool."

At most events on the PGA Tour there are pairings for day one and day two. No matter the scores shot this grouping will play the first two days together. At Augusta it was different. Each day the pairings were created by the scores shot the prior day.

"So now I am in the last group with Lanny Watkins for the second round of The Masters. I am beyond nervous. Now, in my mind I am thinking that I don't want to be the guy that is leading The Masters and misses the cut. I am thinking, 'Jimmy don't mess this thing up.' Instead of playing to win I am playing not to lose. Which was crazy but that was me. Even when I was playing at my highest level, I had doubts. I struggled with it at every level of my career. But now I know that was just me and it was just fine.

"I started slow with a bogey at the first, but I didn't' shoot myself out (Jimmy shot 74) of it. Lanny was backhanding putts and getting mad, but he was playing great. I was thinking to myself, this is crazy. I am worried about making the cut and this guy (Lanny Watkins) is mad because he isn't birding every hole.

"This coach for Villanova's basketball team was as at Augusta that year. His name was Rollie Massimino. Every day before the round he would watch me hit balls and then shake my hand and wish me luck. I will never forget the last day I was going down the 17th fairway and I looked over in the gallery and Coach Massimino was there. I signaled to him and he wandered up to the ropes."

"How ya doing out there pro?" he asked me.

"Coach I am so nervous I don't know which end is up. Then he said something to me I will never forget."

"Jimmy you can't get hit by a car unless you play in the street."

"That quote may end up as my favorite of all time. Once I got to the 17th green I finally knew what he meant. He was telling me not to be scared. He was reminding me that I can't sit back here and watch but I have to get in there and get dirty. Champions get in the street and they feel things that people who walk on the sidewalks don't feel. That is just a fact of life in all areas. I ended up finishing 17th that week and got an invitation back to Augusta.

"So, everything is good heading into the PGA Championship at Crooked Stick. I am playing great golf and then Linda gets sick again in May or June and began radiation again. During that same period, we also we found out that Cissye was pregnant.

"Cissye and I were at Hartford and I had a really good shot into 16. If I could have birdied a few in I could have won. I remember looking into the camera on the 17th hole and saying, 'Linda I am doing this for you. I hope I can pull it off for ya,' or something like that. Anyway, I didn't pull it off, but it was another good tournament. Cissye and I leave there and go to Erie, Pennsylvania, and we get a call from Ed telling us that Linda was not going to make it another forty-eight hours.

"All the joy and all the happiness gets turned around. All the great golf and the applauding fans, that seemingly were an ever-present part of our lives gives way to the reality. Now Cissye and the family who had been there so strongly for me and my career needed me. It was time for me to back up my girl and her family and be there for them.

"I guess I had grown up because I knew it was time for me to be there for them. We had the funeral, and all this was happening the week before the PGA Championship at Crooked Stick in front of all my family, friends and hometown fans. I go to this tournament not thinking about the tournament at all. I am thinking about the Meeks family and Cissye.

"The pairings for the PGA Championship come out and I am paired with Rocco Mediate and Arnold Palmer, the King. The only thing that came to my mind was that Linda walked into heaven and said, 'Listen you have got to do one thing for my family. You gotta pair him with Palmer for the PGA at Crooked Stick.'

"Cissye's dad and her brother are coming and maybe, just maybe, if I play well enough, I can help ease the pain and help Cissye and Keasler mend too. And lo and behold I finished third. I made a putt on the last hole to have the low round on Sunday. Leitzke made a thirty-footer on the last to finish second and beat me by one. Daly wins by two or three. Although many thought he would, to his credit he never folded. Daly was just playing, and his playing was good enough to win.

"The first two days playing with Arnold Palmer was the time of my life. I really, honestly didn't know what to call him. I didn't want to call him Mr. Palmer because that might make him feel old. I didn't want to call him Arnold because I didn't want to insult him. So, I ended up saying 'hey' a lot. It really took the pressure off of playing because I was playing with the king and I wanted to beat him. I wanted to impress him.

"I have this picture of Arnold looking at me as his caddy and I are laughing. We are on the 16th fairway. He looked over and asked, 'I wonder why we didn't play that back tee?' Without thinking I said, 'The PGA is waiting to open that tee until all the bad players miss the cut.' As soon as I said that he hitched up his pants and hit this two iron in there about eight feet and looked over at me and winked. That was Arnold.

Jim's play was steady as much of the PGA Tour season played out. With the last major on the schedule, The PGA Championship coming up, he was excited to play the major in front of fans in his home state of Indiana.

"When I knocked in that putt on the 18th that Sunday I had gone from the worst week of my life to maybe the best. It was golf ecstasy that week. Better than my first win on tour. In front of my home state, family and friends. A great week of something for all of us to celebrate."

Jimmy made $692,000 in 1991. A break out year.

In 1992 Jimmy made nine cuts in a row. "Right after 1991 Bruce Leitzke made a bet. We decided the low man on the money list for the year would have bragging rights for the entire next year. It kept him playing and it fired me up. Every week I was trying to beat up on Bruce."

No swing work---just playing golf.

"Nineteen ninety-two was a fun year. Mary Langdon was born, and we were all traveling around. Golf was great, money was coming in. In 1993 things changed some. Every year I had achieved goals. Every year I had accomplished some of them but not all of them. Cissye and I sat down and made some big goals. I wanted to win multiple tournaments, finish in the top ten on the money list, make the Ryder Cup Team and make one million dollars.

"In 1993, Cissye talked me into calling Dr. Coop to be a part of the team. Early in 1993 I struggled. I missed the cut at the Masters, the U.S. Open and The Memorial. I hurt myself and the injury kind of freaked me out. By late June I wasn't anywhere near where I needed to be. When I missed that cut in Chicago, I still remember saying to myself 'Jimmy you had better get off your pity party and get out of this mindset. I can remember it. I was miserable! I couldn't wait to miss the next cut because I was playing so bad. I don't know what happened, **but I went to the Anheuser-Busch and won.**

"Looking back on it I see that I injured myself and tried to play through it. That was a mistake. But after winning I jumped into the Top 8 in Ryder Cup Points. So here we go. Next thing I know I am at the British Open, tired and not wanting to be there. I miss the cut and go home to Greenwood to rest and reset.

"Here is how strange my mind is. As I walk in the locker room at the British Open, tired and testy mind you, I look up and there is this poster that shows what the other tour players have to do to pass me. I get all worked up about the world being against me and just couldn't get past it that week. That is really why I missed the cut at the British."

After a little time at home, Jim Gallagher, Jr. finished T-2, T-19, and T-10 leading into the 1993 Ryder Cup. Beginning on July 11th of 1993 Jim would play the next four months with a scoring average of 70.37. He won the Anheuser-Busch, finished second at the NEC World Series of Golf, T-10th at The Canadian Open and played in his first Ryder Cup.

Jim Gallagher would travel to The Belfry and under quite odd circumstances and win his final day singles match against Seve Ballesteros. That story is for another time, but here are his words after being a member of a victorious Ryder Cup team and beating the best Ryder Cup player of all time on home soil.

"I felt like I could accomplish anything."

"There were two events I walked away from during my career and was like 'wow.' The Ryder Cup was one of those for me. My performance there was huge to me as a player at that level. Huge. Before I went to England no one was giving me enough credit as a player. When I got back to Jackson, Mississippi, that had changed. I had finally proven to the golf world that I was more than a kid that had dreamt of being a world-class player; I finally was recognized as one."

"After the Ryder Cup of that year I told a reporter that I had proved to the world I could flat play. My confidence after the Ryder Cup was on another stratosphere. Then I go to the Olympic Club for the Tour Championship late in 1993, which was the last event of the year.

"I play with Gil Morgan the first round and shoot 63 to break the course record. Funny thing was the last time I had played that club I shot 87. When I walked in the press room, they start asking me questions about my round and I say, 'Boys all I know is that I am 24 shots better than I was when I was a junior golfer because the last time I played here I shot 87. I was laughing, joking and playing on house money. My confidence is through the roof.

"I remember I had it above the hole on the 18th from the back-left side. It was the same place Payne Stewart had four or five putted from the year before. I hit this putt and it literally held its spot on the top side of the hole, just a dimple from toppling in. I couldn't believe it. But my playing partner Scott Simpson comes over to me after the round and says, 'You couldn't do that again with a thousand putts. In fact, you couldn't two putt again with one hundred putts.'

"Norman makes his way in and can't catch me and an hour or so later I win the Tour Championship. With that I accomplish every goal in 1993. I make the Ryder Cup Team. I win multiple championships. I make more than one million dollars in prize money.

"For me winning always bred winning. I didn't change coaching, swings or equipment. I changed the most on the inside. I put so much emphasis on money and performance early. Later I didn't pay attention to the money. I let go of the monetary achievement. It became more about points or beating other players."

Achievement and Accomplishment are different. Achievement is the realization of reaching a goal. Accomplishment is to finish and complete the undertaking. In 1993 Jim Gallagher, Jr. had finished and completed every goal he had set for himself. That is rare, very rare.

Generally, a list of goals will be looked upon after a season of labor, whether it is in the world of business or sports, and many of the goals will be accomplished, but rarely are they all accomplished. In fact, the real reason goals work is because it aids us in focusing our attention in trying to achieve the little pieces that make up the goals.

Recently a college athlete reached out for some assistance on the mental side of the game. I quickly asked him to write down his top ten goals while at the university. Second, I instructed him to get ten additional pieces of paper. On the top of the page of the first piece of paper I asked him to again write down his first goal from the previous listing of his top ten. Beneath that I asked him to write down ten more goals that would lead to accomplishment of that one big goal.

He did the same for each of his top ten goals. He actually struggled but with a little assistance was able to work through and list not only his top ten goals, but also the one hundred process goals that would lead to the success of the big goals. When he finished, I had one question.

"What did you learn?"

"They all run together, sort of; I mean to accomplish what I want in the classroom requires organization and doing the small stuff each day. To accomplish my goals requires organization and doing the small stuff each day," he replied.

In 1994 Jim Gallagher, Jr. played in twenty-seven events on the PGA Tour. While winless for the year, he did record a lone second place finish and five top ten finishes. He made the cut in sixteen events and finished inside the top twenty-five in all but one of the events that he played. A tie for 33rd at the Nestle Invitational was the only event that Jimmy would make the cut and not finish inside the top twenty-five.

It was a down year for one of the top twenty professional golfers in the world, but it did have at least one highlight, the inaugural President's Cup.

It was a different story in 1995: twenty-seven events played, two events won, two second places, a solo third place finish, six Top 10s, and twelve Top 25s. Of the twenty-two cuts he made that year he would finish inside the Top 25 fourteen times. It was a record setting year that once again proved he was one of the best golfers in the world.

Magically, tragically, or maybe just as intended, it would take Jim Gallagher the next seven seasons to earn as much income as he did in 1995. In June of 1995, in Memphis, Tennessee, he won the last trophy to adorn his trophy case. In full, Jimmy would play the game of golf on the PGA or Champions Tour for an astounding thirty-three years. Over those years he would play in 547 PGA Tour Events, making 306 cuts.

During those 1,706 rounds of golf he would have FIVE career wins, nine second place finishes, nine third place finishes and fifty-one Top 10s. He would be a member of one Ryder Cup Team and the inaugural Presidents Cup Team. That little boy from Indiana who learned to play the game with old coffee cups in his front yard became one of the best players in the world, if not the best player in the world, for a brief period of time.

ONLY ONE SHOT

10

"I AM GOING TO DISNEY WORLD"

Golf lessons and diets don't work for the same reason. It is easy for a child to feel entitled. Are we feeding entitlement or making our children earn experiences? This chapter introduces you to a key concept: The Habit Calendar, the process of using a calendar and some drills to build a really great base for junior golfers. It will open your eyes to a different way of practice with a method that has been proven effective time and time again.

Most everyone can remember the answer to Walt Disney World's famous TV commercial at the end of the Super Bowl. The commercial was simple. The football player was asked: "You just won the Super Bowl! What's next?" The player would joyously shout to the camera: "I am going to Disney World!"

Disney World is really appealing to children. Rewards come easy at Disney World. Kids can eat cookies at 10:00 am and probably get away with it. Kids can devour ice cream for lunch and parents will allow it. There is visual stimulus everywhere, and adventure around every corner. Everyone is welcome to be a part of something special.

In sports, however, not everyone is welcome to be a part of something special. Sure, you can be a fan of a great organization but that will not make you a player. Sure, you can get lessons from the best instructor but that will not guarantee anything but the best information. Being a part of something great requires disciplined, sustained, and correct work. It is really that simple.

Let's survey our children's lives for a second. Mine each have an iPod Touch, loaded with Apps and games. The iPad Santa brought was supposed to be for "educational" Apps only, but now college football games rule. When they start a fire, they do it with a starter log. They have a 35-inch television, teddy bears, a Play-Station, dozens of footballs, swords, a tight rope in the back yard, bikes, trikes, skateboards. We scrimped and saved to buy a house in a neighborhood that is safe for our children.

How about the experiences we provide for our children? Our family does not go to many places (maybe the beach once or twice each year). Often times, my wife and I feel like we, as parents, should do more for our children. Sure, we have been "out West" and, of course, to Disney World, but we feel compelled to take our children to other places for "the experience." In fact, as I look around at our children's lives, I see more items they don't use than ones they do use. Is this normal? Or am I creating a Disney World on a middle class budget?

The harsh reality is that if we keep this pace up, our children might not have time to become great at anything. They will be too busy "experiencing" things to settle in and begin the slow steady art of becoming great at something. Moreover,

when we want our children to "go to karate" they, of course, don't like it. When we demand that they go to their rooms and "study," they put up a fight. Of course, if my wife forbids me to eat ice cream while at Disney World, I would get upset pretty quickly. Wouldn't you?

Disney World is a wonderful place, but its experience should not be lived every day by children who want to be great at a specific sport. Giving you 13 year old a speech on discipline while you play video games with him or her probably will not result in increased discipline. Sending them to their room to work on their putting strokes with a television sitting on the chest of drawers will probably lead to a lack of deliberate practice. Texting constantly on the golf course and then expecting your child to focus on their routines will probably lead to problems down the road.

At the same time, taking out the gas stove and installing a wood burning one probably isn't the greatest idea either. Throwing the video games in the garbage and handing your nine-year old son a wood splitter will probably cause some problems. Taking your daughter's high heels from her closet and replacing them with golf shoes will, no doubt, throw some gasoline on a fire with the ladies in the house.

Diets don't work for a reason. People eat out of convenience and they get fat. At some point, they get so fat they must lose weight. A big problem, however, with squeezing in the workout and changing the diet is that these activities are so far from the normal routine that the individual cannot sustain these activities. So, the diet falls by the way side and the person goes back to eating the way they did in their normal routine.

Golf lessons don't work for a reason. People practice out of convenience and they don't shoot the scores they wish. A big problem, however, with squeezing the extra practice time and changing the swing is so far from the normal routine that the individual cannot sustain these activities. So, the lesson falls by the way side and the person goes back to playing and practicing as they had before the lessons.

Responsibility and relevance work hand in hand. When a child grows up in "Disney World" is suddenly asked to give me 1,000 reps of a certain drill and play 45 holes weekly before their next lesson, they look at me with a confused expression.

Note that I am not passing judgment on what happens in your home in any way. Instead, I want to lay out a plan that you can implement that will take your child from "Disney World" to the "Battlefield" in stages that can be accomplished. So, no worries, you can keep the air-conditioning and TVs plugged in (for now)..

Years ago I was on a research mission. I wanted to know everything there was to know about impacting a golf ball and thinking one's way around a golf course. **The focus of my research now is on what will lead to the biggest gains in performance.** What I have also learned is those who are the best at this game are interested in ways to improve performance. They aren't interested in being a lab rat. They want to play better golf.

One evening I was sitting in a hotel with a player and we were talking golf. "Why do you teach?" he asked. I replied, "Because this game really makes me angry. People think I love golf, but I don't. I want to beat the game." Laughing, he replied, "VJ, you can't beat this game. You can only steal moments from it, and hope you are putting for a million dollars when you do." Maybe he is right. Maybe the game cannot be beaten, but there are some ways that are better than others when it comes to stealing moments from this game.

Over the years, there are definitely ways that lead to bigger gains with developing golfers. The former chapters were laid out for that reason. If you will stick to them you will see some huge gains in your children's golf games and possibly yours. This chapter contains some physical and mental drills that have worked beautifully for many different players. We are going to lay out the path to ease out of "Disney World" and onto the "Battlefield!"

THE HABIT CALENDAR

A centerpiece of instruction for juniors is the habit calendar. It is where the children earn instruction. It is where they earn new equipment. It is where they earn golf balls. The habit calendar should be put in a centralized area of the home, a place where everyone can see it. The "team" (parents and the child) determines an amount of time or a number of reps that should be done daily. The child performs the reps daily and puts an "X" (or whatever they wish) to show the task has been completed.

Pictured above is an example of a child's habit calendar. For a child to create good fundamentals in their golf swing, they must move. Remember, swing changes happen at a cellular level, not a cognitive level. Therefore, it is imperative they not only work on their swing, but they do it often. Furthermore, the skill of becoming responsible for preparing for an event is a learned behavior just like hitting a chip shot is a learned behavior. The habit calendar is the beginning of this **Process.**

The habit calendar above is from a seven year old. He practices a particular element of his swing three minutes each day. At the end of 60 days, he has earned another lesson or golf balls or some type of reward. I often use the habit calendar as a calculator too. T seven year old worked on "shortening his swing" for 60 days—and he even did so on Christmas day! The total time devoted was 180 minutes. You can use the calendar to show your child that doing a little bit every day really adds up.

TThe habit calendar can eventually go away. Sooner than later, you will see a child that feels compelled to work on their swings, or their putting, or their chipping each day. By holding them accountable in the beginning, you are teaching them to hold themselves accountable in the end. This accountability puts a premium on preparation. Before the habit calendar goes away (more than likely it will be around for a number of years), it will be adjusted to work on all elements of the game. At some point, a very mature point, time will no longer matter. Instead the player will practice with intentions that probably cannot be measured with time alone. I should confess, however, that to this day, I personally practice using a habit calendar.

Fundamental Drills

BALL POSITION

Ball Position is a fundamental element to the golf swing. I often remark that ball position can be either a tempter or a teacher. For a young player, ball position is an important fundamental to create a nice weight shift from one leg to the other in a consistent sequence. As golfers improve, ball position hugely affects the path of the club and the curve of the ball. Eventually, a laundry list of swing "complications" can be traced back to the fundamental element of ball position.

For youngsters, my preference is definitely a forward ball position. Two golf balls inside the left heel is acceptable for the beginner, and ball position will become more and more important as they continue in the game. The reason is simple. If the ball position is constant, the weight shift can be consistent. The exercise is simple. Address the ball over and over, (for a pre-determined amount of time/reps each day) making certain the ball is positioned two golf balls inside the left foot.

BALL POSITION + BODY POSITION

A bit more advanced way of learning ball position can be done using a mirror. Here the junior sets up to a ball that is played two inches inside the left heel (the center of the ball) and they also get their body in a neutral position. A neutral position means that their shoulders, hips, knees and ankles are stacked on top of one another. As a result of this neutral position, the ankles bear the weight of the knees, the knees bear the weight of the hips, and the hips bear the weight of the shoulders. This neutral position will place the neck between the feet.

Again, this drill is simple. Walk into your stance looking at the ball—just as you would when you are addressing the ball on the range. Once set, look into the mirror. Check ball position, neck position and joints. Repeat. It only takes a glance to see whether your child is not in a neutral position. Then, of course, you can them see the compensation and make an adjustment. Repeat for the desired amount of time or reps.

GRIP

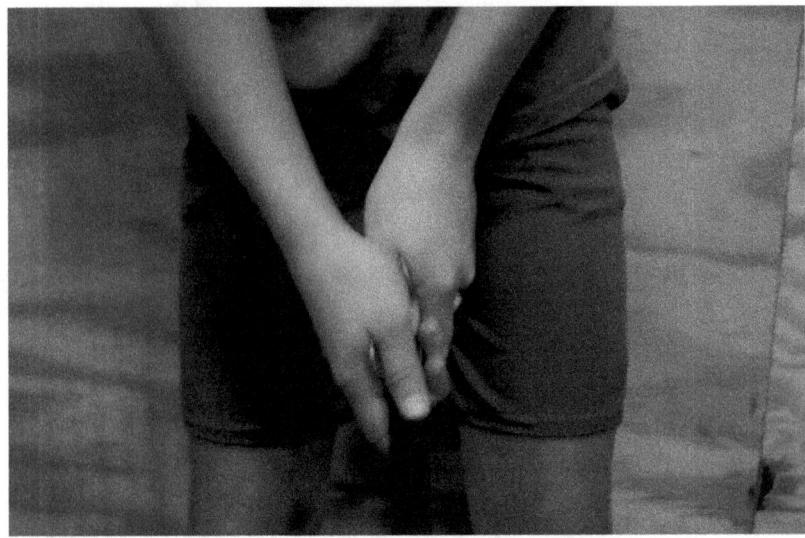

A junior golfer's grip will change and change and change! I have found really no rhyme or reason for it. Generally, the trail hand will get a little under the shaft or the lead hand will get a little too far on top of the shaft. Whatever the case, too strong of a lead hand will inevitably cause a shut face and a digging tendency around the greens. A trail hand too far under the shaft will generally cause a less than desirable wrist release pattern, especially around the greens. Keeping the grip as neutral as possible and as consistent as possible will be a time saver later in their golfing careers.

This drill, or exercise, is generally done sitting on the couch. Again, it is very simple. The goal is to have the "v" formed between the thumb and index finger point (essentially) to the rear shoulder. My preference is for the children to hold a coin between the thumb and index finger because it serves multiple purposes later on. With that said, they simply put their hands on the club, note that they are properly placed and waggle the club a bit. Take the hands completely off the club, and repeat the same task for the desired amount of time or reps.

ROTATION

Give an outstanding instructor a kid that can turn and look out! You may call me crazy when I say this, but an athlete's ability to feel the differences between turning, tilting, and jumping, will ultimately build their swing shape. The reason is power. When an athlete needs to hit the ball with power they will try and generate it. For this reason alone, and the legion of ways a player can figure out a "way" of creating power; copy this exercise on a consistent basis

1) The rear foot is stable. 2) The ankle, knee, hip, and rear shoulder are in-line 3) Arms are extended.

It is really that simple. Ask them to rotate into the backswing and hold for one to two seconds. You will need to do some coaching and it will take a more than a little patience from both you and the athlete; but I assure you it will pay dividends later.

ROTATIONAL THROW

After some backswing rotations and holds it will be time to move into the downswing or through swing. The athlete will love this one, and I would suggest not having anything breakable within twenty feet or so. You want the athlete to be able to rotate thru the motion with stability. If they accomplish this properly, the following look with take place:

1) The lead foot will be stable. 2) The ankle, knee, hip, and shoulder will be stacked. 3) The trail shoulder will finish in front of the hip. 4) The trail hip will finish in front of the knee. 5) The knee will finish in front of the ankle.

Use a mirror to help your young athlete see the finish if needed. The more they use this basic principle of throwing the more they will learn to differentiate between rotating, tilting, and jumping. They will build a physical foundation on which to build their golf swing. Repeat the same task for the desired amount of time or reps.

THE PUTTING STROKE

Use Putting Arc models to create a station of practice where the putter path and face can be seen and practiced. Don't use a ball. Just follow the directions using both the heel and toe of the putter. For a more advanced version of this practice keep the putter head equal distance from the arcs. Perform for the desired number of reps.

Secondly, great putting requires stability. The head moving around is a sure sign that other joints of the body are moving as well. Let's keep it simple for the kiddos and go for the eyes.

Purchase a mirror made for putting (www.theputtingarc.com) and get the athlete practicing two ways. The first way is to simply make strokes keeping the eyes still. The second way is to make strokes using a ball but after the strike, keep the head down long enough to see the eyes. Do this indoors without a target. Perform for the desired number of reps.

PLAY

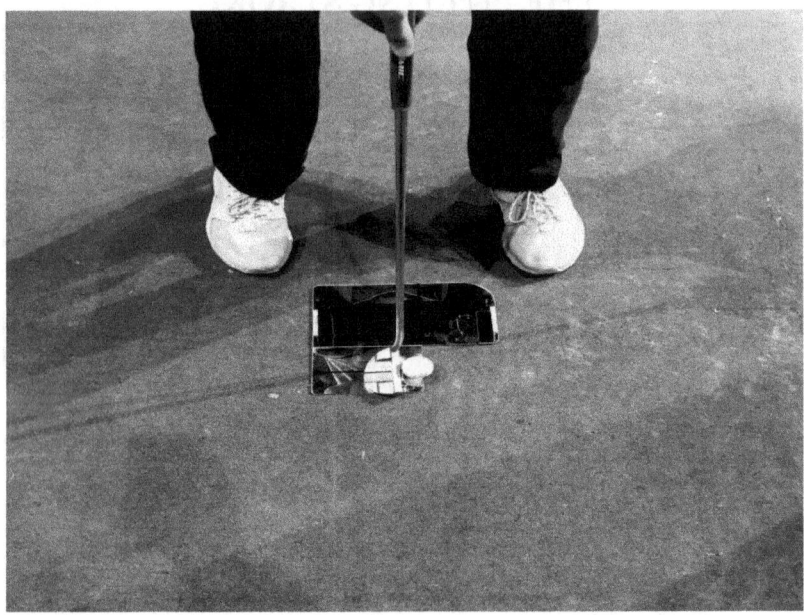

Forget the custom of playing nine or 18 holes of golf. Encourage them, bribe them, do whatever it takes to get them to the golf course and play a few holes—even in the worst weather. Whether it is three holes with a buddy or 18 holes with the club champion, playing golf regularly will lead to huge gains. Keep them on the course regularly and, more importantly, let them have fun playing golf..

The pictures in this chapter were taken in our home for a reason. You don't need a fancy Teaching Center! You don't need a "golf room" dedicated to the sole purpose of improving the golf swing. All you need is some knowledge, motion and intent. Utilizing these physical drills and the mental drills of proper practice is a big part of the foundation. **Trophies may be handed over at beautiful places, but they are not earned there.**

A very, very good foundation for a junior golfer to build upon is:
- A neutral-ball position
- A weight shift that accommodates the ball position
- A steady head and a decent putting stroke
- A stable body when hitting chip shots

Even more important is for parents to cultivate a deeply held belief that motion is necessary for junior golfers to learn how to play golf. This aspect of golf is possibly even more important than helping to cultivate accountability for preparation. Accountability for preparation will eventually be the foundation of their future.

Expecting children to go from video-game playing, sugar-loving creatures to ball-beating athletes overnight is silly. Slowly implementing structure to their lives with habit calendars and simple drills while re-enforcing that preparation is the key to performance is very possible. For the seven-year-old it may be three minutes or twenty-five reps with one drill. For the ten-year-old it may be six minutes or fifty reps with two drills. Again, **responsibility and relevance go hand in hand.**

Also remember there is a big difference between random and block practice. Go back to the analogy in "Underwater BB Stacking." There are many research papers that show that block practice will lead to less retention of the skill. While random practice will be a more difficult and will push your child, it will lead to higher retention. When you see them zoned-in for two minutes and then they walk away, don't start yelling at them. It is fine for them to break it up. One minute of intentional, deliberate, randomized practice is worth hours of "block" type practice with no purpose.

Much of this learning process relates to child development. I do not think age is as important as understanding your child or having the PGA Professional they work with understanding your child. The drills or exercises must be done each day, with the possibility of taking a couple of days off. Children should be held accountable

for doing the drills and exercises. A time period or rep number that is too short is much better than one that is too long. These drills and exercises should be set up to fit nicely into the development and goals of your child. You should also be aware of the number of things the child is working on. For example, my seven-year -old is working on one thing. My nine-year-old is working on two things. Keep it simple. Keep it fun. Be adamant about accomplishing their tasks each day and marking it off on their habit calendar.

The college golfer you see working on their game each day was taught accountability long ago by something or someone. Whether it was a grandpa, socio- economics or simply a desire to enjoy the sport, they learned to be accountable in preparation for the desired outcome. They may have spent a little time at Disney World riding the rides, but they also cleaned up after themselves along the way!

Chapter Lessons:

- Disney World is a great place, but the aspects of therein should not be lived every day by children who want to be great at a specific sport.

- Arm your children with the weapon of accountability.

- Golf lessons work or don't work for a reason.

- Expecting children to go from video-game playing, sugar-loving creatures to ball-beating athletes overnight is an unrealistic expectation.

- Relevance and responsibility go hand in hand.

- Trophies may be handed over at beautiful places, but they are not earned there.

11

REVIVED

A well-watered, fed and sheltered Greek civilization is noted in history for their creation of the Olympic Games. From that time, with very few breaks, the world of sports has grown tremendously. There were sincere innovations that were brought into the separate games that would shape and change them to such a degree that they would become known as the biggest technology advances in the history of sport.

Consider the shot clock in basketball. In 1953 the scoring average for the league was seventy-nine points per game. In 1954, the year the shot clock was adopted, the scoring average was ninety-three points. The shot clock changed the game. But the shot clock could only come into existence because of technology; the players had to be able to see it during play. It had to be big, bright and accurate. There are other examples such as carbon fiber skis, concussion helmets for baseball, instant replay, steroids and composite tennis racquets. The game of golf was introduced to a couple of major changes in less than a decade.

In 1990 Mizuno introduced the first titanium driver. It was named the TI – 110 and while it was cast by some of America's best precision aerospace foundries (Titech, Selmet, Wyman Gordon, etc.) it was marketed almost exclusively in Japan. In the United States, Callaway had branded its name and by the time of the release of the first titanium driver from the company, in 1995, the Great Big Bertha sold like coffee on a cold morning. The first titanium driver in America was actually the MacGregor T-920, but it did not become the king of the fairways like the Great Big Bertha.

Titanium is lighter than steel or wood, which had been the common technology used in drivers and fairway woods. It is also one of the hardest materials known. Now the head could become much bigger, much more forgiving and much harder. Designers could move the club's center of gravity to create different launch conditions that were never possible before. Designers could quite literally change the shape and performance of one of, if not the most important club in the bag.

From 1985 to 1995, the driver played by professionals and recreational players alike changed significantly. With the evolution from wood to metal and ultimately to titanium, it grew bigger (sometimes two times as large), lighter, harder and longer. It alone, changed the game. In 1985 Andy Bean led the tour in driving distance at 278.2 yards. By 1995, it was John Daly at 289.00 yards. By 2000, over 300 yards led the PGA Tour. The driver was only one piece of the story.

One Sunday in 1930, Phil Young, an avid golfer and owner of Acushnet Rubber Processing Company, missed a putt. The story goes that after missing a putt Young was convinced it was the golf ball. With the help of a friend he used x-ray equipment from the hospital and found that his ball was truly "out of round." Young gathered up as many balls as he could, and upon x-raying them he found there was much inconsistency the balls on the market during that time.

While Phil didn't know a lot about golf balls, he did know a lot about production and consistency. The natural thing to do was to spend three years figuring out a way to produce very reliable and consistent golf balls. The first Titleist ball came to market in 1935 and it was unstoppable. Acushnet and Titleist became synonymous and built a huge brand.

Through generations of trial and testing by major companies, the best ball on the market was really quite simple: take a core, wrap rubber bands around it really, really tightly and put a dimpled cover over it. It was such a good design that it was the choice of competitive players for forty years or so. Slowly technologies were created to research and develop ways to actually measure and change the amount of spin a ball would produce.

Once the golf ball leaves the clubface it immediately hits air. The dimples on top of the ball move in the same direction as the flow of air while the dimples on the bottom move in the opposite direction of the air flow. The net result of club impact and the composite of the ball create both the launch and spin conditions of the ball.

The best golfers in the world are really, really good at predicting and executing the launch angle, launch direction and speed of a golf ball. No matter the era of golfer, the best were capable of creating launch conditions that were predictable and consistent. When the spin of the ball changes the trajectory it also changes the distance the ball carries. In very short order this requires the player to make adjustments, whether on purpose or not, to create the same launch and spin conditions they prefer.

The new ball was different. Instead of the core being tightly wrapped rubber bands, the balls had a core consisting one to three layers of polybutadiene (synthetic rubber) which is known for its resiliency or ability to quickly recover its original form after being compressed. Quickly, very quickly, the golf ball changed significantly.

There were and still are well established and enforced rules that govern the modern golf ball. It cannot be smaller than 1.68 inches in diameter. It cannot be any heavier than 1.62 ounces. And it must also meet restrictions on speed, aerodynamics and distance.

In the mid 1990s the Titleist Balata or Maxfli HT was the ball every competitive player trusted. It was a wound ball with a liquid core. In 2000 the Titleist Pro V1 was released to PGA Tour professionals. The new ball simply left the face faster and spun less than the old ball. The newer ball was a three-piece ball with the liquid and the wound rubber bands of yesterday no longer present.

The core of the ball had changed within a decade and completely changed how the ball reacted once compressed. Couple the advancements of the ball and the club together and the core of the game changed.

In 1985 a 280-yard drive was rarely seen. By 2000 there were thirty guys on the PGA tour averaging 280 yards. The driver and the ball, in a remarkable fifteen- year period, had redefined what constituted "a good drive." The ball was not only carrying ten to thirty yards farther off the tee, it was also going four to ten yards farther with irons. In 1985 you played a 450-yard par four. After a remarkable 270- yard tee shot you are still left with a 180-yard approach. That would equate to a driver and a four or five iron. In 2000 if you played the same hole, after a modest 290-yard tee shot you are left with a 160-yard approach. That would equate to a driver and a six or seven iron.

In the case of golf, as most sports, the athlete did not change the game as drastically as the equipment. Without knowing it, Jimmy Gallagher was right in the middle of the changes. He had grown up playing persimmon woods and wound golf balls. Within five years after making the final putt to win the FedEx St. Jude Classic in Memphis, the only "wooden" piece of equipment in Jim's bag would be the tee itself and the only thing "wound" would be his emotions.

After the Wins

In 1996 Jim Gallagher Jr. is one of the world's top players. His wife, Cissye, is pregnant with their third child. His coach, Jim Gallagher Sr., is with him approximately ten weeks out of the year. There are endorsements after the wins. The endorsements are very substantial monetarily, but there is a caveat, to pay for your name they want you to play the new equipment.

"I really never changed growing up. I was a creature of habit and that is part of why I may have been successful. I didn't like change because it had never been normal for me to change." Jim begins.

"I didn't change swing instructors, wives, lives or routines of practice and play. The only thing that significantly changed was the equipment I was using.

"Back then we didn't have cell phones or video to share. When I began to slip a bit in '96, '97 and '98, I didn't really know how much my swing had changed at the time. I really thought it was just confidence and I would play my way through it. It wasn't until years later that I was actually able to see my swing in the early to mid 90's side-by-side with my current swing. I couldn't believe the difference.

"My golf ball didn't react the way I expected it to. Growing up I hit so many shots from so many different lies and positions on the golf course that I knew what it felt like to hit a great shot and a poor shot. That is the reason I have always considered myself a 'feel' player. Typically, if it 'felt' like a good shot it was, and if it 'felt' like a poor shot it was.

"I don't blame anyone but myself when I say this, but my 'feel' of the game changed. The ball and the club 'felt' different. There were shots I hit that I swore were perfect and they would be average. There were shots I hit that I swore were terrible and they were great."

The equipment had changed. The club he trusted on twelve to fourteen holes a day did not look or feel close to anything like the club he had wielded over the previous twenty years. The new golf ball reacted differently than any ball in the history of the sport and certainly different than the ball he had played most his career.

By testament, Jim had always had moments of doubt that he overcame with hard work, coaching and the encouragement of family and friends. So, a poor '96 was not the end of the world for him. By all accounts it wasn't as if those close to him "saw it coming" or "he stopped practicing or caring." It was simply an "encouraging time off the course and a discouraging time on the course." As an athlete it was a tough time. As a human being it was a blessed time.

But the two to three-year period following the '95 season was a storm of sorts. The Gallagher family had always been self-reliant. Senior had passed this down to Jimmy. No one needed to hold his hand on the range or watch him hit every ball, chip and putt. Stick to the fundamentals and what got you there; if you are in doubt practice and play some more. The only difference during this era was the ball and woods had changed dramatically and athletes in the world of golf were getting longer and straighter. Jimmy had to make decisions on equipment.

Jimmy made his decision just as he always had. He went to Greenwood Country Club and the PGA Tour and played the new equipment. "The players around me were getting better, hitting it longer and straighter. I was slowly losing confidence in my way of doing things."

With all the emotions athletes go through to compete, it is important to stay objective as a coach. I have learned this the hard way over the past two decades. The limbic system, emotions and the brain components do not fade with age. Players and competitors get heated, worried, anxious, confident, determined and aloof all the time. The coach or guide does not always have this luxury.

In **1990** the longest driver on the PGA tour was at **279.2 yards**, in **1995** it was **289 yards** and in **2000** the record was **301.4**. Jim Gallagher was roughly twenty yards shorter than the longest hitter on tour in '93. In '94 and '95 he was within roughly fifteen yards of the longest hitters. In '96 Jimmy averaged 277.2 and the longest was 288.8.

In **1997** Gallagher drops to 45th in driving distance at 273.1 yards; the leader was 302 yards. For the first time as an elite athlete in the game he was being outdriven by nearly **thirty yards.**

Statistics reveal a similar story in "greens in regulation." From 1985 to 2000 the leader in greens in regulation for the PGA Tour averaged approximately 71% of greens hit in regulation. (A green hit in regulation is when a player has a birdie putt on the hole being played.) This means the leader on the PGA tour was averaging somewhere between twelve and thirteen birdie putts per round. During Jimmy's two win years he averaged approximately 67% of his greens hit in regulation, giving him twelve looks at birdies per round. In '96 he hits 66.97% of greens in regulation or twelve greens in regulation per round. In 1997 he falls to 63.67 or eleven greens in regulation.

During his winning years Jimmy ranked T-30, T-12, and T-12 in driving distance. By 1997 he ranked 45th. During his winning years he ranked 47th to 69th in greens in regulation. By 1997 he ranked 126th. The storm during this period can objectively be seen as equipment. At the time Jimmy was unaware and emotional; but the reality was that he had never been outdriven by thirty yards and hit so few greens. When he was winning the longest of the long were no more than fifteen yards in front of him and likely did not hit as many greens as he did.

"My expectation went from 'expecting to win' to 'expecting something bad to happen.' In '96 and '97 I had my card secure because of exemptions from previous wins. I didn't let up or try less. I truly stuck to the day-to-day process that had gotten me there.

"In 1996 we had three kids and Cissye was not traveling as much. In 1997 and 1998 Cissye and the kids really stopped traveling as much with me because our oldest was starting school. During this same period Bruce Lietzke stopped playing as much and would soon move on to the Champions Tour. I felt secure on the road with my wife and family, as well as my dear friend and mentor Lietzke. It helped me immensely.

"Lietzke was like my big brother on tour. Because of Lietzke, I became accepted into the group of world-beaters like Curtis Strange and Lanny Wadkins, and I felt accepted into this world-class group. He would always get me into practice round pairings with these players, and I would see how they prepared and how they dealt with competition. I lost my mentor and tribal leader when I lost Lietzke.

"When it began to slip, Cissye and the kids were at home. She needed to be home with the kids and I understood that completely. Fellow pros don't want to spend time around someone who's struggling during practice rounds and preparation.

"From '93 to '96, I felt like I should have won twice as many tournaments. Then in '97, '98 when the ball was going everywhere and shorter than some of my contemporaries, I wondered, 'What is going on? How did I go from thinking I should win two to four times a year to yelling 'fore' off of two tees per round?'

Performance in sport is very similar to performance in any other part of one's life. It is a presentation of skill. The skills we carry into our lives are important to us. Sometimes it is our job that demonstrates our skill set. Sometimes it is those we coach that demonstrate our skill. At desperate times, our skills begin to reflect how we see ourselves functioning in life.

This is Jimmy's world in '97 and '98. His skill in life was his performance on the golf course. He was accustomed to being a "CEO" or "President." He had proven to himself and to others that he belonged in that position. Redemption for the athlete comes only when goals are achieved. When performances yield no redemption, people often look to the past, not only to console themselves but also in hope of exchanging their present self with their old self.

"In the back of my mind were the expectations. I felt like I needed to be playing like a "tour championship winner" or a "Ryder Cupper," and I just put more and more pressure on myself. At the same time, I had no one looking at my swing or fundamentals. My Dad begged me for years to understand the swing more so that if something happened, I would know how to fix it. I never wanted to hear much about mechanics.

"I remember still being very good at recovery shots because they were second nature to me. I could hit a little punch cut or a hook around a tree. I could hit it high or low, but my swing didn't feel second nature anymore. My golf swing felt contrived and untrustworthy.

If my performance was less than desirable, I found myself looking for an excuse. When that didn't remedy my poor play, I would blame it on the way I felt. On a few occasions my dad, Cissye and a few others would offer their opinion on my swing. I would have none of that.

"All those years growing up in Marion, playing mini tours, practicing at PGA National with all the resort people, I had never made excuses about my play. I just went to work and made the best of my situation. But in that period, I did start making excuses. It wasn't smart. It wasn't smart at all."

Gary Player once said something along these lines, "You have to work very hard to be a natural golfer." When you see a good golfer, you are looking at many, many hours of concentrated work. In the upper levels of professional golf, players are spending anywhere from fifty to one hundred and fifty hours yearly with a coach.

In the mid 1990s most parents didn't watch junior golf, much less collegiate golf. In a sense it was very normal for a player to try and work it out on their own. Jimmy and other players of that era were the last generation of great players to approach playing, practicing, testing equipment and training alone.

"The smart thing would have been to stop making excuses first. Then take weeks off and go back to Marion and spend time with my dad. But I thought I could play my way out of it. I kept thinking I could just play my way out of it and I couldn't.

"When I look back, all those excuses and decisions were basically out of self-pride and fear. The pride comes when you remember how the trophy felt in your hands as you lifted it up, but now you are standing on a tee hoping you don't hit anyone with an errant tee shot. Less than five years earlier I was sitting in the Oval Office with the president and now I am looking for my lay-up shot on a par five.

"The fear was the unknown. I never liked mechanics and didn't think of golf as a technical game. I didn't know if I could ever get it back if I started looking at my swing. By then people were using slow motion VHS and video. Coaches were out there with camcorders, recording swings. That scared the hell out of me. I knew how to play golf. I knew what a great shot felt like. When it came to the swing, I always just trusted my dad's eye, so I was fearful of all that swing stuff."

The equipment in the game of golf had undergone massive changes with the ball and driver in particular. Technologies with video were growing and becoming more present. Jim Gallagher Jr's mindset caused his struggles to become more pronounced. He wanted the old feel and confidence served up really quick. What he needed was some hard work and time. But the scores were defining him at this point. "I was letting golf define me. I was letting how I performed now compared to how I performed before define me. If you are an athlete, you simply cannot let how you perform define you." Jimmy says.

"Athletes are known for how they perform and that is fun. But when the athlete begins to build their identity around how they perform the trouble starts. I was never the most popular kid in high school or at the University of Tennessee, but I was more popular because I could play golf. As an athlete it is sometimes easy to begin to feel that people like, love or accept you because of **how you perform rather than who you are.**

"Athletes and those close to them should keep an eye out for this. Sometimes the athlete is mistaken in thinking that people only like them because of how they perform. Sometimes the athlete is correct. During my lowest points in the late '90s I felt like I was letting the world down by not performing well.

"I am still as competitive a guy now as I was when I was younger. I love to compete and watch competition. I had four children attend college; two of them as student athletes. I have always parented them the same. Telling them to do their work... that they have to work for things in life. Cissye and I also remind them of who they are and that just being themselves is fine.

"If there was anything positive that came from that period it was this. Have big goals. Don't make excuses. Work really hard. Pray and make the best decisions you can. But after it is all done each day leave your work at work. Leave your score at the golf course. Leave your grades at school. Remember, it just fine to be you."

By 2003 Jim Gallagher was no longer an exempt member of the PGA Tour. The benchmark season of 1993 was a distant ten years in the rearview mirror, and he was 42 years old. "I made a statement when I first got on tour that I was going to play until I was forty-years-old and then retire. I was going to make enough money, have my family and retire. The year I turned forty, I lost my card.

"A buddy called me in 2003 and asked, 'Do you remember how you told me you were going to be retired by forty with enough money and a great family? I just called to congratulate you. Awesome job.' I just smiled. It was amazing really, to have someone call me and have a *totally different outlook* on the situation than I did. While I was going through athlete melt down there was this old friend, watching me and thinking, 'Jimmy is getting it done exactly the way he said he would.' It was a very self-reflective moment for me."

A New Goal

"I went to work for USA Network full time from 2002 to 2006. I was just a basic, on-the-ground-guy who would walk with groups and do a bit of live reporting and that was very natural for me. At the Tucson event in 2003 they moved me to a hole announcer. I had never done that and was completely out of my comfort zone. I did my homework and worked hard at it though. In April of 2003 I got a call that I would be doing the 18th tower, which is one of the 'spotlight' jobs in network golf announcing. One month later I was interviewing arguably one of the best athletes in all of sports during a career-defining moment."

Annika Sorenstam was born in October of 1970 in Bro, Stockholm County, Sweden. Before retiring at the end of the 2008 LPGA season, she won seventy-two official LPGA Events including ten Major Championships. With eighteen more additional international titles, Annika Sorenstam tops the list as a female with the most wins to her name.

Sorenstam's record is amazing: over $22 million in prize money won, Player of the Year on the LPGA Tour a record eight times and winner of six Vare Trophies (given to the LPGA player with the lowest seasonal scoring average). She was the first woman to shoot 59 in competition and competed in the Solheim Cup eight separate times. Sorenstam shifted the paradigm of what a female athlete could achieve in a sport. So much so that in 2003 she became the first female to compete in a PGA Tour event in six decades.

"I approached my television just as I had approached my game," Jimmy begins. "I wanted to always be prepared. I knew what Annika was doing on the LPGA Tour would impact women's golf forever and I had a feeling what she was doing at Colonial could really impact the game itself.

"My job that week was clear: be a neutral television announcer covering Annika Sorenstam. I watched her all week. She was a professional for sure. She handled the media and expectations perfectly. She handled her game on the course and the spotlight of golf so well.

"On Wednesday I went out to the Pro Am, introduced myself and walked the entire eighteen holes with her and the Pro Am partners. I said 'Hi I am Jim Gallagher Jr. and I will be with you all week. I have played this course a million times so if you have any questions, I will be happy to answer them.' There was a lot of pressure on Annika that week. There were some players calling it a publicity stunt. There were players in complete favor for it. There was speculation about why she was playing. There was speculation all over the place. It just grew and grew during the week. It was really the story in all of sports by the time she hit the first tee shot."

There were record crowds that week. Annika would shoot 71, 74 and miss the cut by four strokes. Amid all the chaos of rows and rows of people and cameras, Annika Sorenstam performed like the champion she was. Amid all this was Jim Gallagher Jr. as well.

"It was my fifteenth event as a television announcer, I think. I know she was nervous because I was, and I wasn't even playing. There were people standing in trees and just groves of people in the gallery. She played really well over the thirty-six holes and hit it well enough to have made the cut.

"In addition to calling the action from the course while following Annika, it was my job to interview her after the Friday round. While I was waiting for the interview her agent asked me what I was going ask her on live television. He was just trying to protect her, I am sure. I told him not to worry about it that I was a former player and was there simply to let the world hear her side.

"When she came out of scoring, I will never forget putting my arm around her and said 'Hey we are all proud of you. You played great!'

"Annika responded, 'Thank you but please don't make me cry on live television.'

"I looked at her and said, 'If you won't cry, I won't cry.' We both shared a laugh and then the interview began.

"What people need to remember about Annika was she put herself out there. I was there, face-to-face with her, and it was a huge moment in golf. She was a competitor and playing that event was apparently her 'Mount Everest.' I was completely impressed and learned one important lesson from her: **champions are driven by internal desires to overcome and achieve**. She embodied that her entire career and it was especially evident that week. Annika had more to lose than gain from the outside looking in. But from where she saw it, she had more to gain than to lose.

"My perspective of her after that week was cemented. Annika was a very special athlete. She demonstrated the same characteristics that great male athletes demonstrate when performing. I wanted to portray that side to everyone that watched the interview. I wanted them to know how well she performed and under what circumstances.

"Over the years at USA I interviewed so many good people and amazing athletes. Annika, I remember so well because of the significance of the event. In my new job I quickly learned, or was at least reminded, of one of the perks of my hard work. All that hard work, while not intended to lead me into television, had given me perspective on what it means to accomplish things in life. I understand the things athletes and business leaders have to give up and overcome to succeed. This understanding made it easy for me to interview them.

"TV kept me in the game, really. I still loved the game of golf. Being able to still be around it was really good. It was also a challenge. Just as in the game of golf I was constantly being pushed to be better. I practiced hard, learned as quickly as I could and did my homework so that I could do the best job possible."

Jim Gallagher Jr. was still playing a bit too.

Off the Course

From 2014 thru 2018 he played in nineteen events on the Champions Tour. But there was much more golf played away from tournaments. In 2010 Jimmy shot a course record 58 at Greenwood Country Club during a round with the guys. That 58 would be the second time he broke 60; the first was in 1983 with a 59 at Meshingomesia Golf and Social Club. The Gallagher family would vacation at Old Waverly Golf Club in West Point, Mississippi, and they played hundreds of rounds at the Greenwood Country Club.

Jim's story as an athlete was only a part of the story during this period of his life. He was also a husband and father. Outside of the world of golf, the Gallagher family had continued to raise their family and build their lives in the small town of Greenwood in the fertile Mississippi delta. Their children would grow into teens and ultimately into adults. It was a busy time but there was still plenty of golf played by the entire family.

Cissye Gallagher, Jim's wife, won the Mississippi Women's State Amateur in '86,'87,'88,'93,'94,'97,'98,'99,'01,'04,'06 and '15; a record twelve times. She also competed in the USGA Mid Amateur in '06 and the Senior Amateur in '18. Jimmy would caddy for her in 2006 in which she would make match play.

His oldest child, Mary Langdon Gallagher, would play college golf at Mississippi State University from 2010 to 2014 on a team that was at one point ranked number one in the country. She married Caleb Hardman and had their first child, a boy, in 2017. She would also win the Mississippi Women's State Amateur.

His son Thomas Gallagher would attend Mississippi State and receive a degree in marketing. After college he would be a member of the team that opened the doors at Mossy Oak Golf Club in West Point. The Bryan family brought together architect Gil Hanse and outdoor and hunting lifestyle company Mossy Oak to create this unique club known simply as "Nature's Golf."

Kathleen Gallagher, their third child, would play collegiate golf at Louisiana State University (LSU) from 2015 to 2019. As a member of the women's team she would play in every college event as a female student athlete and receive her degree in marketing. She too would win the Mississippi State Women's Amateur.

Elizabeth Gallagher, their youngest child, would attend Mississippi State University as a freshman in the fall of 2018. In high school she would be part of student government and a member of the soccer and basketball teams.

"My life has been very blessed," Jim Gallagher begins during a late afternoon chat at his home in Greenwood. "The game of golf has changed as much over the past thirty years as my life. The length of the courses, the distance the ball is being hit, the technology and coaching staffs that are at events. The game is now a year around game as well.

"But for all the differences though, the game is still the same. I was a junior golfer. I was a college golfer. I was a winner on the PGA Tour. I was a Ryder Cup Team member. I had to learn to compete and learn to win through rigorous steps before eventual wins. It is the same steps now as before.

"When my career on the PGA Tour began to change, Tiger Woods began his assault on professional golf. Arnold Palmer and Jack Nicklaus brought golf to the masses. Tiger Woods brought the game to the world. Globally, the game's popularity exploded because of Tiger Woods.

"The guys competing now grew up watching him mash drivers down the middle of fairways. They grew up studying his game or being coached by people who studied his game. They grew up being able to see their swings immediately because of technology.

"There were great athletes when I was playing. I just think there are more of them now. Athletes from all over the world now know they can become a player on the PGA Tour. Tiger Woods, I believe, is the reason for this. His statistics are just amazing. He overpowered everything and had the precision to back it up. The generation competing now grew up thinking this was the standard.

"These are the reasons you are seeing younger and younger guys and girls winning at a professional level. They are climbing the same steps as those who came before them. They are learning to play. They are learning to compete. They are learning to win. They are just doing it at a younger age. They are doing it quicker than any generation before them because of technology, better coaching programs and because they are just like us; they love to compete.

"When I look back on my career and look at the careers that are budding and developing on the PGA and LPGA Tours, I can't help but think of my parents. There is so much that goes on during those developmental years. The parents and the mindset of the home is so important. Just take for instance, specialization.

"There are tons of data and statistics now that demonstrate early specialization in sports is a bad idea, but I have seen in real life the effects when it goes wrong. Not all kids can commit to one sport at ten or eleven- years-old. Not all parents are good at balancing the wins and losses or ups and downs that will occur. I hope parents will allow their kids to play multiple sports if the child wants to.

"Professional athletics is not easy. People talk about 'Getting paid to play golf,' but there are also a lot of airplanes, hotels, moments missed with family and daily discipline that is involved. Even at a college level, the student athlete is giving up a lot of what many of us would call the 'college experience.' The lifestyle is different. It is not nine to five Monday thru Friday with a couple of weeks of vacation.

"I only hope parents will look at this from a healthy perspective. Let the kids play sports. Let them play as many as they like. By the ninth or tenth grade they may need to dwindle it down to two or three sports. By the eleventh grade or their senior year if they can play two sports, let them.

"If a kid is going to play professional athletics there will be signs. You don't have to worry about that. But everyone's road to professional athletics is different. Some may get there earlier than others. Some may get there later than others. But one thing is for sure, before and after professional sports there is a person. That person needs to be comfortable in their own skin growing up and that person needs to be comfortable in their own skin after the lights are turned off.

"I love the game of golf and I love competing. I have played it, shared it with my family, covered it as an announcer and built a lifetime of memories around the game. For that, I am deeply thankful, and I hope everyone who plays will enjoy the memories they build around the game.

"At some points in my life I fell in love with trying to be a better player, a better husband, a better dad, a better Jim Gallagher Jr. At some points in my life I fell apart because of how I was playing, or how I was acting as a husband, as a dad and as Jim Gallagher Jr. None of us get there alone. We all have to reach out, to branch out and to learn.

"I have watched players turn 69s into 75s all my life. I have only watched a few players turn 75s into 69s. Life is much the same. Rarely did I have my 'best stuff' when I won on tour. I spent too much time looking for 'the best stuff' when I was playing poorly. That is the hard part. The key is taking advantage of the resources around you. The key is not being too stubborn to admit when you are wrong. No matter how good we get or how good we think we are; we will need solid resources, or we will need to be solid resources. We will also need the ability to take advantage of it by listening and learning.

"There is no quick answer. I was awesome at listening about six months before I played great. I was terrible at listening about six months before I played terribly. The keys are having resources and constantly listening. Our society today is all about the here and the now. Fix it now. Let's go try this. That didn't work so let's try this instead. That mentality along with the 'Blame Game' was the mindset that hurt my career the most.

Great golf is a bundle of skills just like life. A dad or husband can make a bunch of money but not spend time with their kids and ultimately not be a very good dad. A golfer can hit the longest straightest tee shots in the game but not chip very well and end up not being a very good golfer.

"Golf is a test of small-group communication. Most of golf is spent with two or three other people in your group. The smallest and most important group will be your family and your coaches. I wouldn't have made it past *go* with Mom, Dad and Cissye. They were instrumental in my life. Sure, I got beat up as an athlete over the years but so did they. They cared too.

"I am a firm believer there are lessons learned from both winning and losing. In life and in sports we really only have two options: to be humble or to be humbled. Humble people listen. Humble people make a plan. Humble people work the plan. Humble people compete and learn from it.

"Set those goals high but achievable. Build a plan to get there. Get humble and get to work."

12

RANKINGS

You know us. We like to know the score. We have high school beauty/beau competitions. Actors and musicians even have their own award shows. Every school celebrates its valedictorian and salutatorian each year. Even our taxes have a type of system of ranking so the more that is made, the more is paid in. In fact, we sometimes don't even have an interest if there isn't a ranking or scoreboard lit up.

There was a time when I was one of several assistant coaches on my two boys' little league team. It was early on with them being seven or eight years of age. During the three weeks of practice leading up to the season, the stands were a ghost town. The kids would come out, learn a few things, and wear us as coaches out without even a comment from a parent. The first game did one thing that practice did not do; it turned on the scoreboards. The stands filled up, the parents and extended family came out to support their kiddos' respective teams, and the concession stands opened.

Scoreboards and rankings are a part of the fabric of our world. The one thing we all ask is that it is fair; or if it is not fair, we at least want to know why. After all, in America, freedom and democracy are valued. A place where a man or woman can go from rags to riches in one lifetime would be our motto. So, we don't do well with others making decisions on "how good" or "how average" we are, and without hesitation, we will turn venomous if that is dealt to our own children.

Rankings in golf are important for several reasons, the first being an accepted ranking system sets the rules. Without an accepted system, it would be nearly impossible to know where we stand in the population of golfers that we compete against. Second, as we all know, a sixty-four at one golf course is not a sixty-four at another golf course. In fact, with golf being an outdoor sport in which we are not in control of the pins, wind, weather or height of rough, a sixty-four at the same course shot at different times is not even the same sixty-four. Third, rankings enable coaches and the various appointed team and tournament selection committees a statistical and comparative method to make decisions on who to recruit or allow in a tournament.

Rankings are also important to understand for several reasons, the first being the fabric of the modern world with online information and computers in all our pockets. It can be a shock to learn that what we value as very good play doesn't move us very much in rankings. Second, tournaments cut into our time and financial resources. It is always better to know the progress associated with good performances before we load up everyone and travel a couple of states over. Finally, as with all systems, those who understand how to use it to their advantage will do so. There are ways in golf to spend thousands of dollars and not move the rankings needle. There are also ways in golf to spend the same dollars, with the same play, and shoot up the rankings.

The hard truth is that rankings do, in fact, matter. College coaches and tournament selection committees have other jobs and a family of their own. The easiest and most practical way to spot talent is through rankings. Personally, I will share with you that I have evidence that youth athletes should play a tournament schedule mixed with tournaments they are favored to win, some very difficult to win, and some that would be impossible for them to win. The diversity of such a schedule challenges their ability to win, to compete, and to learn to play at a level that may be above what they have seen. But there will come a time in your athlete's development that rankings do very much matter.

The evidence is clear that most parents do not pay attention to rankings early enough. The parents who do pay close attention to rankings early are often ridiculed or talked about among other parents. For me, as a parent, it was a difficult mountain for several reasons. The first was my kids played tournament golf because they LIKED playing tournament golf. We were literally having a good time. At around thirteen years of age, it became apparent there was a system inside the system. Junior golfers were beginning to play vastly different schedules by fifteen years old. With this knowledge, our family had to shift a bit. Mom and Dad had to educate themselves on rankings so they could be better guides. That is the reason so many parents get behind. They, for all the right reasons, are guiding their kids to improve and play well, and the good golf will take care of itself. While that is the truth, it is only half of the truth. The truth is play well in the right tournaments, and the good golf will take care of itself. When the kids can't get in those "right tournaments," that is when the rankings begin to feel unfair.

Over the next pages, I will explain to you the understanding that I use to this day. In advance, I will not suggest it is the "best way" for everyone. With that said, it at least is a system and understanding of rankings that will hopefully arm you with enough information for you to build your own blueprint for schedules and tournaments.

In junior golf, there are several tours all over the country that advertise and host golf tournaments. All the scores from these golf tournaments feed into Junior Golf Scoreboard. Junior Golf Scoreboard brings all the rounds, tournament champions, fifteenth place finishes, and the rest to one area of cyberspace. This is very handy for college coaches and selection committees, so here is how Junior Golf Scoreboard works. Junior Golf Scoreboard uses three criteria for rankings. First is how the player scores versus the difficulty of the course. Second is the strength of the field. The stronger the field, the more opportunity for upward progression in ranking. Third is the finish in the tournament. We take them one by one below.

1st: How well does the player score versus the difficulty of the golf course when playing in tournaments. This accounts for 65% of the ranking. So, score versus course rating. This is not against 72, but the golf course's rating. A golf courses course's rating is created by another system when the golf course is designed and the conditions in which the players are competing. It will have a course rating (example, 75.4) and a slope rating (example, 125). The course rating is calculated via playing length and obstacles of a golf course. The slope rating is a score given to a course to determine its difficulty

2nd: Strength of field. The lower the number shown on Junior Golf Scoreboard, the stronger the field played. This accounts for 25% of the ranking. The strength of the field is determined by the individual ranking of all the players in the field. There are many tournament fields.

3rd: Finish in the field accounts for 10% of the ranking computation. It's based on number of players and the strength of field in the tournament.

Junior Golf Scoreboard's system of rankings is like that of professional tours but alters some because field sizes for junior events fluctuates. Their ranking program and website (www.juniorgolfscoreboard) are very straight forward and inclusive. By finding a player of interest, you can quickly understand the schedule they are playing and the scores they are shooting. This type of knowledge can be important in laying out the schedule of your junior golfers.

A couple of suggestions. Number one, don't sign up and just look at how your kiddo is ranked. While it may be important, it is the least important piece of information you want. What you want to do, as early as you can do it (after the age of ten), is look into the future a couple of years and begin to understand the path of those who have gone before you. Number two, start early and share the information so your junior golfer understands there really is a scoreboard. Over the years, what I see causing the most frustration is players getting sixteen years old or so and then really getting into the rankings. A suggestion to show them JGS and in a conversational manner at a younger age could go a long way. It is a much better idea than showing them at seventeen or in a confrontational manner. Finally, it is important to note that a scoring difference under the course rating (which is shown in Junior Golf Scoreboard as –.59 or –7.59) is an important stat. I would suggest the evidence I have supports the idea that every junior golfer who has gone on to play Division 1 golf has a scoring difference of –2.0 or more. Scores certainly do matter most.

Rolex Rankings, which is an AJGA based ranking system, is commonly referred to as "AJGA's Ranking System." It is a bit more complicated as it has its own pathway based on performance inside the Rolex Rankings. While the Rolex system does consider large national events, most points and rankings will come from an athlete's performance in AJGA events in contrast with JGS (Junior Golf Scoreboard) that considers all tournaments, no matter the "tour" they are played on. So, let's get in here.

The American Junior Golf Association or AJGA uses a "star" system to get into events. Stars can be earned by performance in primarily AJGA events. It can simply be the idea of "stars" by comparing it to points. Essentially, a player must have enough points to get in the tournament, and once they are in the tournament, they are competing for the trophy and points, which are referred to as stars. There are three basic AJGA events: Junior All-Stars, Opens, and Invitationals. Open Events are true to their name. They typically have a qualifier before the event in which anyone can try to earn a spot in the tournament. Junior All-Stars and Invitationals are a bit different as they don't all have qualifiers. Invitationals are true to their name; they are playable by invitation only.

The AJGA mirrors the PGA Tour in some ways. A player on the PGA Tour (as we discussed in Gallagher's story earlier in the book) may not be eligible for certain events even as a PGA Tour member. At present, the PGA Tour has "elevated events" in addition to regular season events, Invitationals, and the majors. The player's past accomplishments on the course open up doors to what could be viewed as a "tour within the tour." The elevated events and majors have bigger purses, so once you get within the top fifty in the world rankings and play an elevated schedule, it is difficult to "lose" your card. Change the language around a bit, and the AJGA is very similar with its construction.

The AJGA uses stars to prioritize rankings. A Top 5 or Top 3 finish (boys and girls) will give you a status of Fully Exempt. However, just as on the PGA Tour, Fully Exempt does not mean you have access to any event on the AJGA Tour. It means you are in that category, along with others. In many instances, the entire field will be fully exempt players, so a player with eighty stars will not get in. And then there is a point structure.

The point structure can be understood by looking along the top line. You will see 200-point tournaments in the first column and the points provided to the finish. For example, first place receives 200 points and second place receives 120 points. Strolling over to the 70-point tournament, first place will receive 70 points and second place will receive 42 points. This point structure was not widely circulated or understood during our junior golf era. It slowly became apparent that not all "Junior All-Stars" or "opens" were equal. Homework had to be done to truly understand the point total the players were playing for.

Important Notes Here:

- 1st place receives 60% more points than 2nd place.

- A 10th place finish in a 200-point tournament = 28 points

- A 10th place finish in a 100-point tournament = 14 points

- A 10th place finish in a 50-point tournament = 7 points

While the AJGA does mirror professional tours with its "tiers" of tournaments and "payout," it can be confusing and frustrating. The evidence I have suggests the earlier you start the process of accumulating stars and understanding the AJGA System, the better. The AJGA Tour has a history of having the best players competing on tough golf courses, so it is a college coach's pick. The reason? Going to one place and seeing a bunch of talented kids play is a no brainer for recruiting. If you are diving into the AJGA for the first time with a junior golfer at fifteen years old, it can be difficult to break into the upper levels. In that case, there is evidence that playing in qualifiers and playing well in the event is the only option.

I would also suggest the AJGA carries a social status among teenagers. Often, I have seen a player believe that playing in an AJGA event is something special. The reality is it is an opportunity. A Top 10 or Top 15 may feel good, but just as all the "tours" and "rankings" in golf, first place is paid very well, second well, and by the time you get to an arbitrary tenth place, it will be a small percentage of the perks enjoyed by first or second.

AJGA Rankings Summary:

- PBE or Performance Based Entry
- The AJGA initially uses the "star" system to get into events. Stars can be earned by performance in AJGA events.
- There are three basic AJGA events: **Junior All-Stars, Open Events, and Invitationals**
- It "costs" 4 stars to play in an Open.
- It "costs" 1 star to play in a Junior All-Star.
- Invitationals are "invitationals," so they don't cost anything.

Open Events Explained:

- Largest single-category AJGA event with 65+ run per year
- Uses PBE or stars to sort the applicants
- Usually has one-day qualifier
- Can play in five events per year

Open Stars Given Per Event:

Top 5 – Fully Exempt (which means you are at top of list for future Opens)

- Top 10 – 12 stars
- Top 15 – 8 stars

- Top 25 – 4 stars

- Top 50% or make the cut – 2 stars

Junior All-Star Stars Given Per Event:

- Champion – 12 stars

- Top 5 Boys – 8 stars

- Top 10 Boys – 4 stars

- Top 20 – 2 stars

- Top 50% – 1 star

Invitationals:

How the AJGA Rankings System Works

- 1st – Points are given on a per event basis. A player's total points for each event is then divided by 6. If you don't play in six events, you are still divided by 6. So if you play in four, you will have two "0s" that will be used to divide into your total points.

- 2nd – The ranking system is on a fifty-two a week rolling cycle. So your finishes will stay on AJGA Rankings for fifty-two weeks and then roll off.

- 3rd – Players are rewarded for playing stronger fields just as in Junior Golf Scoreboard. Invitational AJGA Events and historically strong junior events such as US JUNIOR, WESTERN JUNIOR, ROBERT TRENT JONES GOLF TRAIL JUNIOR, PGA JUNIOR, etc. are awarded 200 points. All other championships receive between 20 and 100 points.

In 2019, Cohen Trolio qualified for the US Amateur through the USGA's thirty-six-hole qualifier. The US Amateur in 2019 was at Pinehurst, and after two rounds, he had made match play. As a sixteen-year-old, he went on a run through the rounds of 64, 32, and 16. In the quarterfinals, he won his match 1 up. It may have been before the quarterfinal match or before the semifinal match, but somewhere in that period, the press figured out that Cohen did not have a WAGR ranking.

WAGR is the World Amateur Golf Rankings. There are others such as scratch players and data golf, but as for right now, it appears WAGR still holds the position as the most used and viewed Amateur Ranking system. Case in point, PGA Tour University, which was unveiled in June of 2020, uses a "filtered version of the World Amateur Golf Rankings" to establish the ranking list of the top male collegiate golfers. Essentially, WAGR is the ranking system of amateurs extending beyond junior golf.

WAGR rankings include male and females from 102 countries and approximately 7,500 players. Amazingly, there are more than 6,000 ranking tournaments played in 104 countries that are totaled on one site. The WAGR system, like all systems, must change with the time. Currently, to become a WAGR ranked player, a player must receive a finish position of at least 6.5 ranking points in a tournament. Unlike Rolex or JGS, WAGR covers two years or 104 weeks in the rankings.

The older WAGR system used a system with Elite, A, B, C, D, E, F, and G events. In the older system, Elite events were akin to the Asia Pacific Am, International European Amateur Events, World Match Play, US Amateur, and British Amateur. A events were essentially Sunnehanna, Western, Northeast, Walker Cup, Pac Coast, and other events of similar scale. B events were the equivalent of Terra Cotta, US Junior Am, and Terra Cotta Invitational. And the list ran on and on.

While the newer version requires 6.5 points to get ranked and 4 points accumulated during the year to keep your ranking, the older version was based around finishes. For example, a Top 40 in a A event would get you ranked, and a Top 20 in a B event would get the job done. This system would end up with G events, such as the legendary Press Thornton Future Masters (tournament won twice by Carter Loflin) requiring a win to go get WAGR ranked.

Without an adequate WAGR ranking, college players can get caught in the middle. There is evidence that getting WAGR ranked early and playing in AJGA Invitationals and national junior events can drive a player's ranking up the ladder. Upon entering college, these same players will have access to stronger fields. This will give them the opportunity to move up the WAGR ladder quicker than players playing a weaker schedule.

On the opposite side of the coin, players good enough to play collegiate golf but who don't have a history of performing at an elite level in junior golf often get WAGR ranking much later. The college or university they play for may not play as strong of events as others (there is the 500 rule in NCAA Golf), and thus they will move up the WAGR ladder slower.

Players want to play in good events and win them. Systems are set up to assign a number or point average to each event that will promote a simple idea. If a player is playing a hard course, with a lot of great players, and they win, they will receive significant points. A player playing an easier course with a few good players will receive fewer points. It is after all, a system.

National Junior Events such as Jones Cup Junior, Western Junior, PGA Junior, USGA Junior Amateur, and AJGA Invitationals will be played on harder golf courses and with the strongest fields. Regional Events such as SJGT, SNEDS Tour, Hurricane Tour, and their counterparts will be harder courses and stronger fields than state events. The score shot is most important. Where the athlete shoots the score (aka the golf course difficulty) and who is playing in the tournament (strength of field) will always matter.

There is a Mason Jennings song, "Pittsburgh," that has the lyrics "Are we high enough . . . to clear the trees," and this type of thought has its place in the world of rankings. I expect by now it is apparent that rankings are needed, and it is clear the system of rankings will work both for you and against you. While this chapter lays out the path of rankings with JGS, AJGA's Rolex, and touches on WAGR, it is meant as an introduction. It is my hope with this introduction that you will be able to have an educated picture of the system before heading into it.

I cannot leave you before revealing this evidence I have collected for the past two decades. If the system of rankings is ignored, it will be frustrating. I have case after case of the late teen (fifteen- to seventeen-year-old) who could be called a "late bloomer" who is frustrated, and their family is frustrated because they can't get into events. I also have evidence that discussing this with your teen early, allowing them to understand the basics of the system, has benefits. It is okay for the youngster to know a "system" is grading them as they compete over the years. What is disheartening for the teen is winning high school state championships or local tournaments only to find out they really don't matter to the system.

With that said, remember, "Good golf takes care of itself . . . but externally it is rewarded by what tournaments and courses it is played on."

13

STORIES

Hierarchical goals are an individual's compass. Whether we believe they are gifts given from God or destiny is not a concern, or it could be said that where these hierarchical goals come from is a different conversation of debate. However, it is absolute that a person who desires to live a hedonistic lifestyle with all the trappings of that path are destined to put more energy, effort, and time into different routes of personal experience than a person who desires to live a faithful lifestyle.

These hierarchical goals will give direction to outcome goals. The determination to create these outcome goals will become performance goals. The desire for certain performances will lead to process goals. These steps done willingly, mindfully, and repeatedly will lead toward the achievement of the outcome goals but not in a linear fashion. There will be moments of doubt, chaos, commotion, and what we would call in the south a "big ole mess." During these moments, what we rely on the most are stories.

Stories are a center point of our culture. Those who make it through the chaos, sometimes achieving the exact goals they hoped, will return to their communities, towns, states, and countries and communicate the experience through one of mankind's most amazing forms of communication, the story. Stories come after the goals are set. Stories come after the plan to create the goals is applied. Stories are relied upon when we don't know what else to do.

In 2025, Division 1 athletics will wander into an unexplored, historically significant time. The apparent reason is because of Name Image and Likeness or NIL. In 2024, the court ruled in favor of the plaintiff (which is a consortium of former and current athletes) who argued the NCAA rules that banned players from profiting from their performances in name, image, and likeness (NIL) was a violation of antitrust law. Reportedly in May of 2024, the NCAA and US's largest Division 1 conferences settled the allegation for $2.8 billion. Athletes playing Division 1 sports between the fall of 2016 and spring of 2023 are eligible for their part of the $2.8 billion, which comes to roughly 400,000 students.

In essence, NIL was passed by the NCAA stating that collegiate athletes could now make money from the commercial use of their name, image, and likeness. Reportedly, the language of the whirlwind $2.8 billion settlement of 2024 allows schools to elect themselves to an agreement allowing revenue sharing with student athletes from a collection of $22 million per year. In principle, the Division 1 universities owe their part in the $2.8 billion, AND if they want to continue to be competitive among their peers across the country, they will raise $22 million each year (in house) to pay athletes. In effect,

Pandora's box is now open. Student athletes are getting paid.

Amateur athletes for decades have been given the benefit of the doubt for substandard performances because they were, after all, amateurs. While many entered collegiate sports with professional level skills and treated their amateur sports as a professional business, there were many who did not. College athletics was as much about development of people and athletes as it was about winning trophies. However, when the prominent power of currency and capital enter the picture, the older story of college athletics immediately changes.

In 2025, the money paid to athletes will roll out the inverse side of being paid for playing a college sport, which is a limit to rosters. While the NCAA has always had scholarship limits for each sport, there has never been ROSTER limits before now. In previous years, a women's golf team may have had any number of (probably averaging about ten) players on the roster while the NCAA only allowed six full scholarships. For men, the NCAA allowed for four and a half full scholarships, BUT there were no roster limits. Accordingly, a very smart college athlete who was a late bloomer could get a spot on the roster and be developed without costing the team a dime from their budget via academic scholarships. Or in another instance, a young athlete the coach really liked (and the athlete was a fan of the coach) could be given a walk on spot to develop into a starter for the team.

There have been thousands of student athletes over the years, and each one of them has a story. The stories vary as much as the personalities and characters themselves, and it doesn't take long for them to share them. The stories you will hear generally have a consensus that collegiate sports pushed the athlete to use discipline, discernment, grit, time management, and ultimately grow into the man or woman they currently are. The stories that are told lay out a positive foundation for many during the questionable and wonderfully free years that lay between being a teen in the home of parents and standing in your own home as a mid-twenties adult. Stories which are layered with growing up, maturing, prioritizing, hard work, hard-won wins, and hard-fought defeats.

The number of professional athletes or those who attempt professional athletics is universally smaller than that of collegiate athletics. The stories, which are harder to find, are a very mixed bag. Of course there are legends with the grandest stories of all. Of course there are tragic stories as well. Professional athletics is more direct, more bottom line oriented, with front offices sometimes making decisions that are very, well, let's call them professional. The decisions generally equate, as do the stories, with more of a monetary character. In the case of golf, you will find players who chased their dream as a professional golfer, and quite often the word money will come up.

Previously, the stories between collegiate and professional athletes will not share the same character of "currency." When in college, it could be assumed most students are maturing into adults who understand the impact of money. In professional sports, the impact of money is understood because they are typically adults who are participating, at least in part, because of the money it does or could generate. That is the nostalgia with the early days of the PGA and LPGA professional golfers, as they played the game more because they loved it because the payouts were generally so low compared to a business lifestyle. One could wonder if the stories of collegiate and professional athletes will be that different in the future.

The roster limitations will be positive for the best. Fewer players on a team. More one-on-one time with the coaching staff. The opposite side of the coin will be fewer athletes will get the opportunity. The opposite side of the coin with those who don't produce may be replaced.

The Division 1 programs that opt into the $22 million profit sharing will be paying student athletes, which will be a financial positive for the best athletes. On the opposite side of the coin, it could generate more "front office" decisions, leading to replacement of athletes who are not producing on the sports field. It could border on the collective consciousness of fans, players, and spectators as semi-professional sports.

It is important to understand the NCAA did not create any new regulations for Division 2 or Division 3 programs. With the roster limits at nine, and possibly lower at some schools, for Division 1 programs, does this mean that more players will move into non-profit sharing Division 1, Division 2, and Division 3 programs? Does it mean more athletes will move into junior college programs to possibly get picked up? Does it mean a caste system reclassification with mid-tier Division 1, and high-level Division 2 will be the next "Division 1" with Division 1 profit sharing programs becoming semiprofessional programs? Whatever it ends up meaning, there are no roster limitations for these Division 2 and Division 3 programs, so they will operate under the old rules.

The story of collegiate sports will change. What will not change is the story of sports. Sports brings with it goals, sometimes collective goals and sometimes individual goals, that get carried out on the playing field. This conflict of winning versus losing creates chaos. The chaos creates a need for order. The chaos brings nervousness and sometimes anxiety. The order brings a plan to accomplish the goal. The order brings emotional flexibility to deal with the swings of momentum. The order brings the determination, grit, faith, and willingness to be courageous. The story handed down by athletes over the coming decades will still involve these very important characters.

With the changing environment of collegiate sports, there will be so many opinions and stories. The story I want to leave you to ponder is this. A young athlete, whose path in life is not known, is given a gift. The gift is a love for the game of golf. The game and their love for it is a vehicle for the individual along their path of life. Along that path, God has placed the hope (order) and the fear (chaos) inside the gift for the athlete to develop into the man or woman that will be needed to travel the adventuresome path God has planned for them.

Everything unknown or not yet gone through or possibly around the corner brings with it hope and fear. It is the ability of us through faith and toil to bring order. To subdue the fear. To make the unknown known for not only ourselves but for those who come behind us. As parents of athletes, you will face this new environment of athletics. What story will you tell? Stories are powerful. Don't let someone (even me) influence your story.

14

A THING OR TWO ABOUT PRACTICE

For twenty-four years, I spent nearly twelve hours daily on the south end of a practice tee, or on the golf course, in Clay County, Mississippi, coaching the game of golf. My steady diet gives me Sunday and most of Monday off. For most of those years, Sundays served as a day with the family and playing golf or light practice. Mondays are more reserved for keeping the house and yard to at least standards of a "good neighbor."

From the early 2000s until 2015, I would spend roughly two months on the road coaching. It would vary between two tours mainly, the PGA and Korn Ferry Tour (at the time the Web.com Tour) with time spent out there and then back home. By 2015, I had a choice to make as a coach because some youngsters here at home really loved the game and were at an age and skill level where they would need more time to come to form. Since 2016 or so, more of my time has been spent teaching and coaching from "home", elite junior events, and amateur events than on the PGA Tour. I tell you all this not so that you can stalk me, but rather to give you a picture of my life so that you have a better understanding of the evidence I will share on practice.

Practice as a verb is to "perform or exercise repeatedly or regularly in order to maintain or improve one's proficiency." It is standard in our culture that a "driven" person will be seen performing actions in a repeated fashion to improve their proficiency at whatever it is they are "driven" to perform. The artist draws. The farmer tends to fields. The baseball player fields the balls. The person who loves God attends church. I have had athletes tell me they need to practice, that they should practice, that they have already practiced, but I have also had athletes tell me they are practicing too much.

As a coach, I have seen practice be abused, manipulated, and manifest anxiety in athletes. I have seen players use practice to not get better at a skill per se, but to regulate their conscious mind and get the "monkey" in their head to stop talking. Practice, well, it can be as complex as humans are. I would liken practice and music in similar fashions. Musical artists tend to reflect, through instruments and voice, the world they ARE PERCEIVING. There is no doubt that we all construct mental boxes or constructs that give meaning to our home, neighborhood, state, region, and life. This is a part of personality, its tendencies, and how we separately perceive the world and give rise to such diversity in music as Pearl Jam, Sturgill Simpson, Kid Rock, and Jelly Roll. All are Americans, growing up within 2,800 miles of each other (that is the distance from Atlantic to Pacific) and living as free people under the Stars and Stripes, but they certainly have different perceptions of the experiences their lives have brought to the table. This same abundance of perceptions and personality are brought by athletes—I will speak about golfers because golf is what I know—to practice. There are ideas of practice that have been handed down such as "doing the work" or being "willing to put in the hours" that I have evidence of being quite the opposite of what is important about practice.

The limbic system is discussed in a former chapter so that we can all understand that being "emotionally sabotaged" is both real and being done by us (not the sport). A part of this system referred to often as the sympathetic and parasympathetic nervous systems plays a key role in practice. The sympathetic nervous system is the "fight or flight" response. The antagonist of the sympathetic nervous system is the parasympathetic nervous system, the "feed and breed" or "rest and digest" response. Practice is not as cut-and-dried as doing the reps and getting better, and we all know this. Going into practice with the sympathetic nervous system on fire would lead to practice being much different. Practice with a person who is constantly giving you feedback, whether positive or negative, and practice is different. Practice requires some form or order to be, well, practice at all.

When an athlete is "driven," there are always two hierarchical items present: chaos and order. In fact, getting to the goal is, in effect, getting through chaos by following a path of order. So why is it that "doing the work" or being "willing to put in the hours" comes out of the mouth so much quicker than "getting the mind in the right spot to do the work" or "providing a focused and playful mindset to the hours of practice ahead of you," which seems to never be uttered? Our mindsets matter, and they matter as much as the physical effort of practice itself. The evidence I suggest is simple; I have yet to see physical practice move a person from a poor mindset. Order comes from the mind.

Is it possible that we should wade off into the weeds for a bit? I will answer that for us, yes. Practice for an athlete is sacrifice. Work for an adult is sacrifice. Studying for an academic is sacrifice. We must understand this basic truth to really understand practice. Practice is a form of sacrifice. And when I am speaking of sacrifice, I am drifting behind delayed gratification. We all know it works. We all know that delaying the current appeasement of our whims always pays itself forward down the road. Practice is sacrificing the time we have today to create skills that will pay us more in the future. Practice is work done today that will pay us in the future. It is a form of delay of gratification in sorts, but the "magic" times have an elixir that create immersion into the practice so playful, cohesive, creative, and innovative that the act of practice is gratifying to the athlete.

Let's take a step further into the weeds. Assuming that a gift is being given to you, does it matter the attitude the giver of the gift wears? Or assuming a gift is being given by you, does it matter the attitude the receiver of the gift wears? Of course it does. There is something about us that we all know—it is what's inside that counts a lot, or even more than the gift. It is where the gift is coming from. The gift alone is great, but being given something by a grateful person is really the icing on the cake. In fact, if we each search through our memory enough, we will probably stumble across a moment in our lives when someone was offering us a gift with a hateful heart, and we probably turned it down.

Now we will not turn this idea into Scripture. But we all know that God measures the heart of men. We all know there are stories in the Bible contrasting the gifts given to God and the heart that is giving those gifts. So, I ask now, is showing up for practice because I have to the same practice as showing up because I get to? Is "doing the work" or being "willing to do the work" with an angry, frustrated, "here we go again" mindset really going to get the juices flowing?

So, this chaos in practice, where does it come from? The evidence I have points to several places. The most common is a poorly structured plan or what some might call "banging balls." The evidence I have supports the hypothesis that athletes need to know what they "will be doing" in practice. The application of this is reasonably simple. In a cycle of practice, an inventory is taken and sections of skill acquisition are emphasized. It could be fundamentals or motion or shots. The inventory prescribes a step-by-step approach to anchor the player's focus. This plan of improvement is written out and/or videotaped for the athlete to follow. The second most common mistake comes from not knowing "why" they "are doing" the practice. As a coach, I know all too well how easy a player can become burdened with too much information. With that said, even the simplest plan from the most simple-minded coach to a willing athlete will still be a challenge for the athlete. Knowing "why" they "are embracing the change" is very important. Visual evidence is often required here. Evidence for the athlete in the form of images, rates of rotation, and shots generally work the best.

Practice can be broken into three basic components. There is practice that is meant to calibrate. There is practice that is in "direct conflict" to a current habit. There is practice that is meant to challenge. Calibration in practice is to focus on current skills to maintain them. This is very typical during events with elite players. Nothing new is being introduced, and the reps are about calibrating ball position, timing, alignments, and a myriad of other items depending on the athlete. Practice that is in "direct conflict" of a current pattern can also be seen with elite players. The "feel" is often very different from what is "really" happening during a motion, so an athlete will use what looks to be exaggerated motions in rehearsal as "feel" that is in direct conflict with the less efficient pattern. This direct conflict practice is seen more with the motion involving speed than slower patterns and is seen further from competition than calibration practice. Finally, the challenge portion of practice is used very often to anchor the mind and body and hit the shot. This form of practice can be seen with making a certain amount of five footers or players hitting shots on the range going through full routines while hitting shots. Challenges in practices are meant to invoke the same process that athletes will go through in competition.

So within the recipe of practice, we now have some very often overlooked ingredients: the mindset we practice with, calibration, direct conflict, and challenge. But what of the emotions or feelings we want during practice? Do we want to practice with the emotions associated with being athletic or technical? Creative and innovative or systematic and by the book? Alert or relaxed? We could go on and on. But the point is what about defining the "emotion" or "feeling" you want to achieve throughout a practice session. Often overlooked, yes, but that doesn't mean it isn't important. If my back were to the wall and I were asked, "So what emotions do I need to achieve in practice?" it would be a rather easy answer. Your optimum mindset in practice will give you the emotions you associate with achieving immersion. It is not for me to suggest what that is, but I can certainly tell you what it isn't.

It isn't anger or a fragmented plan. A mindset of consistent and organized plans to accomplish in practice is helpful. As a coach, I have been a part of a player's team when there were too many voices in the athlete's ear. This invariably leads to the team becoming fragmented in the direction the athlete needs to go and creates frustration, anger, and a disconnected plan. Strive for a mindset of unity.

The mindset typically isn't a subdued or too serious of a mindset for many, especially junior golfers. A mindset that is spirited, good-natured, and even humorous works much better. As a coach, I have been in sessions where there was no room for teasing or humor. They are stale. Early in my coaching years, I had the lucky break of working with a player who was a member of the PGA Tour. It was a big deal for me at the time because those guys were the best in the business at moving the ball around. This athlete always exaggerated their "zones of error" and was jovial about the changes in motion I suggested and he implemented. Being playful, good-natured, and spirited is always a better bet than being too serious or subdued. Don't mistake playful with silly. Playful is working toward excellence done with good humor.

Any mindset that decays confidence and focus because the mindset is fixed is a poor mindset. "It was the same yesterday as it will be today. I simply can't change it." Is a mindset that I combat constantly as a coach. "So, I don't quite have it yet, but I am getting closer." That mindset I have witnessed winning at an elite junior level, college level, on the LPGA Tour, and the PGA Tour. There is a tremendous difference between "I can't do it" and "I can't do it yet." A mindset of progress and advancement.

A mindset that centers around the participant all the time is exhausting. It is a fact that an athlete must be selfish enough to sacrifice other things to be successful, but they don't need to cross the line into "it is all about me." Many great players of the past generation learned the game by caddying and thus observing the swings they were looping for. Going to PGA Tour or LPGA Tour events often leads to better golf immediately following. The point is that observing others doing things that are cool does two things. One is it gets your mind off "you" so that you can observe and learn. Two, it can inspire. Any athlete who loves the game was inspired by it and mimicked their heroes in the beginning. So taking awe-inspiring observations and turning it into "Me! Me! Me!" is never a good idea.

A mindset of authorship and being the originator is certainly better than that of a slave and doing it for someone else. Don't get me wrong, I am certain that I have coached great players who worked at it for a bit because of someone else. But I have never coached an elite athlete who didn't demonstrate they truly believed they (along with God) were the authors of their future. That they could pave their road or be the originator of their own success.

I coached my two sons all their junior golf life. It was very difficult. I had friends in the business who I would call on at times when I knew the kiddos were tired of me suggesting what or how to improve a skill set. The subject matter of "what to do" wasn't the problem. The problem was we were losing the culture of working together. Our mindsets were shifting. When

I say "our" mindsets, I do mean both theirs and mine. I have always been an organized coach, so they didn't have to experience fragmented plans or too much feedback, but I did lose my humor after the same conversation twenty-six times. I did experience mindsets of "well, here we go again" as opposed to "you cleaned it up a bit, now let's keep going." I am a good coach, and the boys did lean into me a bit too much at times to "fix it" when the only way, all the time, is for the athlete to be the author of their own success.

As a coach, I had other good players, really good players, around. I coached players who were on Palmer Cup, Curtis Cup, and were 1st Team All-Americans. I coached players on the PGA and LPGA Tour. My two boys saw me doing this. I had access to some of the best coaches in the country to send video and describe my coaching points. As you can see, as a parent, I had a host of supporters, and it still got really hard. Parents will say, "Hey, you tell them what to do and I will stay out of it," but that is not realistic. When my wife or I was four states away from home on Easter, we were certainly not "staying away from it." When our heads hit the pillows at a Hampton Inn the hundredth time that year, we were certainly "in it."

So as a parent or as an athlete, you are going to be "in it," and the mindset you bring to practice is going to anchor learning, growth, and potential. The evidence I have supports a playful, good-natured, organized, "I am going to get it" mindset brought to practice sessions is significant. Observing very skilled players, practicing with very skilled players, playing with very skilled players, and letting their play (or maybe yours) inspire yours without constant comparison I have evidence of being profitable to attaining goals.

So, when working out your practice plan, remember this thing or two about practice. It is not always "what" we practice that is important. Often, it is "how" we are practicing the "what" that is more important.

While I was close to closing this chapter with the above, I would be awry if I did not take practice a bit further. There is amazing research coming from the technology of today in the world of the brain. There is none that interested me more for a period than that of brain waves. The evidence that "every person will experience the same mood with the same brain waves are present" really caught my eye. I know that based around our personality types and perception of the stimulus in front of us, we can all be in slightly different "arousal states" or "moods." But the evidence of electrical impulses being present in ALL OF US during times of despair, happiness, or innovation was quite suitable for my intellect. The "Hz" (hertz) refers to cycles per second, which is the way brain waves are measured currently.

Gamma waves are the fastest (40 to 100 Hz) and are associated with insight and clarity. Beta waves (12 to 40 Hz) are typical of us being awake and critical thinking. If you have ever "grinded" on something, you were experiencing beta waves. The trick with beta waves is that if you are always grinding, it can lead to excessive stress. Alpha waves (8 to 12 Hz) are experienced when deeply relaxed. Alpha waves are the gateway between the conscious mind (our filter) and the subconscious mind (our innate or intuitive actions) and achieving a state of immersion where the mental noise dissipates, which will occur after alpha waves show up. Theta waves (4 to 8 Hz) are associated with deep relaxation, intuitive insights, and immersion, leading to enhanced learning. Delta waves (.5 to 4 Hz) are there in deep sleep and restorative processes.

The research points to the idea that alpha brain waves, at or around 7 to 8 Hz, are associated with deep immersion that some would call "the zone" or "flow state" where we experience an altering of consciousness that is highlighted as an optimal performance. This scientific evidence is mind-blowing. Despite what we may believe, the evidence suggests the way you feel when you are "deeply relaxed" is a better state of learning, skill building, and performance than when you are "grinding." You may need to read that again. You may need to jump on Google really quick and fact-check it.

I have certainly had hints of this along the years. Donald Stokes was one of the best amateur boxers I ever saw in the ring. I remember seeing him multiple times before fights, and he looked so relaxed—like the way I look in my favorite chair on a Saturday night relaxed. It stood out to me because of all the stimulus going on around the gym at an amateur fight. Then I heard about Tom Brady taking a nap before his first NFL Championship; the nap was twenty to thirty minutes long, and he reportedly woke up only twelve minutes before the team went onto the field. What about the story of Rory McIlroy sleeping late on the day before his PGA Championship win? McIlroy said to the media that he slept so long he arrived only thirty minutes before his tee time. Coincidence?

Rick Sessinghouse, the coach of Colin Morikawa, is quoted saying, "Neurons that fire together wire together." What this means is the more time you spend in an excited state, the more you will find yourself in an excited state. The more time you spend in a relaxed state, the more you will find yourself in a relaxed state. After all, we often become what we repeat, from our state of mind to the traits we carry into the world.

As a parent, I was present during many of my children's practice sessions. Especially when they were youngsters and pre-teens, my attitude or mindset was that of the judicial ruler. After all, when children are at that age, you and I are the cops. As a parent, you will be present too. Your mindset and "temperature" of the practice will have an effect. Replace "grind" with "relaxed." Replace "me" with "wow." Replace "You can't" with "Be decisive, you just haven't yet."

There is much to be done with fundamentals, efficient motion, technique, shots, and competing. There is much to be done with organizing and calibrating the practice. There is much to be done with processes and challenges. All of this will be done with mindsets and those electrical impulses moving through our most northern organ. Turn on some good music, be jovial, be organized, and be a damn good parent/coach.

15

EPILOGUE

Recently, a close friend and I had an in-depth conversation concerning the "business" side of golf instruction. We went back and forth with scenarios and solutions for nearly an hour. At one point I asked him, "Is your business really this complicated? Do you really have to learn all these different approaches to getting your employees to perform?" Without batting an eye his answer was, "Yes."

The ability to learn is necessary for success. After all, aren't we all driven? The ability to learn, however, does not just drop from a cloud. All of our "Eureka" moments come after hours of intense problem solving. The generation of children that will tote your last name around will need to learn these same lessons. That is, they will need to learn how to learn.

The environment they learn in is very much up to you, the parent. Golf is a vehicle for learning. For that matter, nearly every sport is a vehicle for learning. **Keep in mind that your children can learn from their performance or they can learn from the process.** Your child can learn that they are accountable for the performance (outcome) and adjust their preparation (process) after they are emotionally sabotaged. Preferably, your child can be held accountable for their preparation (process) and see the competition (outcome) as a means of demonstrating their preparation

As you know, strategic planning starts with communicating with your child. Often, children and parents do not talk about goal setting until the children are in high school—which is woefully late. Think back for a moment about your own life. How many things have you wanted to be? Personally, I wanted to be a professional soccer player, a receiver for Joe Montana, a world champion boxer, and a Hall of Fame professional golfer. Did I accomplish any of these things? Did you accomplish all of your goals? But think of how empty we would be if we never had any goals.

Discuss "Goals."

The great thing about discussing goals early and then building a process to obtaining these goals is that children slowly learn to deal with failure. Slowly, day by day, they will wrap their arms around the process and embrace it. They will slowly be taught to become a champion through the process of failure.

Here is my suggestion. Sit down with your child and ask them to define a "goal." Chances are you will hear something like "To try to win something." Or you might hear, "To try and be somebody." You may even hear "Score a touchdown!"

After this conversation, explain to your child the difference between an **Outcome Oriented Goal, a Performance Oriented Goal, and a Process Oriented Goal.** An outcome goal is winning or achieving something. It is defeating the competition. A performance goal focuses on improvement in performance. An example of such a goal is holing ten putts in a row or hitting three draws on command. Process goals focus on improving form, movement, and strategy. While outcome goals are usually completely extrinsic, process goals are completely intrinsic.

Here is an example of an outcome goal: To win the state amateur championship. Here is an example of a performance goal: To average 74 in tournaments. Finally, here is an example of a process goal: To spend five minutes each day working on ball position in front of a mirror. Note again that the player is not in total control of either an outcome goal or a performance goal. Players are, however, in complete control of a process goal.

The reason I suggest that you discuss different goals early on with your children is that most children (or people) don't understand the differences among these goals. They don't understand how these three goals are interrelated. They don't understand which goal should come first. They don't understand the process.

Often times, the parents do not understand the process well themselves. Both outcome goals and performance goals are what many will call "practice." The goal is, of course, balance. Balance between achieving the outcome, seeing the performance increase, and a commitment to the everyday process goals. Parents must be aware that the temptation is always there for the outcome goal to take over. When that happens, the performance goals become too important and players easily stray from the process.

A Story

Jim's story gives us a peak behind the curtain into a world where many, many goals were accomplished. I asked Jimmy, during our last interview this question:

"If I were to go back and time and walk up to a twelve-year-old Jim Gallagher Jr. and say, 'Hey I want you to tell us how all this ends up, what your life will look like when you are forty-five years old.' If that little guy heard his future, would he be satisfied?"

"I would have been shocked. I guess I thought he could do it but, I guess I never 100% believed it until I won on Tour. That little boy was always trying to prove that he could do it. Growing up I was the second- best player in the state.

"When I got cut from the high school basketball team in the 10th grade, I thought it was the worst thing that ever happened to me. When I look back on it now it was the biggest reason I became successful in golf. In Indiana basketball ruled, and everyone wanted to be on that high school team.

"Putting on that purple and gold uniform and walking into that gym with seven thousand screaming fans was just as much my dream as the guys that made that high school team. You have to be careful because that stuff can begin to define who you are. Growing up if you made the high school basketball team you were the 'Big Man on Campus.'

"In my culture growing up if you didn't make that team......to a sixteen-year-old Jim Gallagher that meant I was not that good at basketball. I was devastated. That was my perception.

"If you walked up to me when I was in high school and told me what my future looked like I don't know if I would have believed you. All I knew was that I wanted to go to college and compete. Just a chance to be successful in golf was all I was looking for really.

"I think playing college golf against some really good players was most important for my development. My freshman year was great. I played great. My sophomore year I got mono and didn't play as well. My junior year I played great again. My senior year I didn't play as well. It was a lot like my professional career.

"Growing up and competing as an athlete is full of peaks and valleys. Everyone has them. The trick is picking the right wave and riding it long enough. For me the peaks of my career were an amazing time for me. The valleys of my career really knocked me down.

"But that twelve-year-old kid you told that too would have run back to his house really, really happy."

As a coach I have found one thing to be very true; the lofty goals and milestones that I have reached are never what I thought they would be. My perception of coaching a junior golfer onto the PGA tour was not the same as when that reality came to fruition. In 2018 I had two players on the Web.com Tour, one on the PGA Tour, and one on the LPGA Tour. They were all adults that I had taught and coached since they were junior golfers. They were all from my home state.

There was a distinct contrast between my perception of that happening and the reality of when it happened. Goals and milestones in life don't take into account any emotions but joy and accomplishment. Goals and milestones are full of celebration but, they are created by discipline, hard work, attentiveness, long hours, constant planning and implementation. To me that celebration comes from discipline. That joy comes from hard work and attentiveness. For goals to be reached there must be plans and implementation.

As a coach it is apparent that parents have questions about sport specialization. I hope we given you perspective and also discussed the evidence that has been compiled by those that study such things.

As a coach the five Ws and the H of practice are apparent. "Who" should I take lessons from? "What" should practice look like? "When" and how often should an athlete practice? "Where" should practice be performed? "Why" are some athletes getting better and some not? "How" should we go about shooting lower and lower scores? It is my hope that we have given you a perspective that helps you order "practice" so that it doesn't begin and end on a driving range.

Conversations.

Let's look at two imaginary conversations. The first one is my attempt to summarize how we could see such results to the survey. The second one is my attempt to summarize what I would like to see in an attempt to build the process underlying the behavior of champions.

First Conversation.

One day, a parent asks the child, "What are your goals in golf?"

The child responds, "I don't know. Maybe to get better and maybe win a tournament?"

"Ok, great," responds the parent. "Maybe you could aim at playing college golf?"

"If I can get good enough, sure," says the child.

"Well right now you are playing two sports. By age twelve or fourteen we expect you to pick one sport if that is okay," says the parent.

"Okay," says the child.

The parent begins to talk about setting up a plan. "Now in order for you to accomplish your goals, we need to set up a plan. In order for you to get better at golf, and maybe win a tournament, where do you think you need to spend most of your time?" asks the parent.

"Hitting balls on the range!" says the child.

"Absolutely," agrees the parent. I can't think of a better place for you to practice and get closer to your goal of getting better and winning a tournament! Now how much time do you think we will need to get the job done?" asks the parent.

"Maybe three times a week for thirty minutes?"

"That sounds great. But what are you going to be working on?" asks the parent. "Playing," says the child.

"Well you can't play at the driving range, can you?" asks the parent. "I mean hitting balls!" says the child.

"There you go! You are going to be hitting balls. We will go play some on the weekends," says the parent.

"Wow, fun! Should I chip and putt?" asks the child.

"I don't really think so. Why don't you just concentrate on hitting balls and building a good swing. I have a surprise for you if you practice too!"

"What is that?"

"I am going to get you lessons so that your technical skills of swinging the club get better and better. You are going to build yourself a great golf swing I bet! Are you excited?" asks the parent.

"I sure am. Thanks!" says the child.

Does this conversation really sound like the way for this child to accomplish their goal? Note that this conversation has produced an outcome goal. There are no performance goals. Just a few performance goals go a long way. The process goal is to go to the range three days each week. At the range, however, what will be emphasized? From the conversation, we really do not know.

Second Conversation.

"Hey, let's talk about golf. What might be one of your goals?" asks the parent.

"To get better, I guess. If I get could get better, I would like to win a tournament!" says the child.

The parent asks, "What kind of tournament? A state sanctioned tournament, a local tournament, a club tournament?"

"I don't really know. I guess maybe a local tournament, and then maybe a sanctioned tournament," says the child

"Okay. Well let's make winning a local tournament your big goal. We will change it to a state tournament when you accomplish the first goal. Now what scores will you need to shoot to win a local tournament?" asks the parent.

I think "38 or 40," says the child.

"I agree. Why don't we put shooting 38 as one of your performance goals? We will take you to Baskin Robbins when you accomplish it!" says the parent. "In fact, we will set 46, 44, 42, and 40 as performance goals. Each time you accomplish scoring a new low, we can all go to Baskin Robbins!"

"Awesome!" replies the child.

"Now what do you think some of the things you are going to need to work on to accomplish your performance goals?" asks the parent.

"My swing. Hitting the ball straight and a little longer. My score...." says the child.

"Yes, that is right. You are going to need to improve everything. Your mind a little, your technique a little, your short game a little, your strategy a little. You get it, huh?" asks the parent.

"Kinda," responds the child.

"Well now we need some goals called process goals. These goals are not quite as fun, but they sure are important. These goals are things that you must do every day. When you do them every day, you are accomplishing your performance goals. Now I know you are not a huge fan of having to run with the track team, but that running is really helping your body get stronger. I also know you are not a big fan of gymnastics or karate. But, both of these activities are making you stronger too.

When you do these other sports, you will be building a strong and athletic body to bring to the golf course. You will need to work around all these activities, so let's plan this out," says the parent.

"Is that why you make me go to that stupid gym? I always wondered why," says the child.

The parent chuckles, "That is right! Now you will have three days each week for the next two months to work on your golf game. Let's break it up," says the parent. "First you need to play. Just improve your strategy of playing golf and getting the ball around the course. It is not so important what you score. When you go out to play, I want you to concentrate on what you are thinking. Don't worry about where the ball goes. After it goes where it goes, it is where it is. You can't go back and change it. Find the ball and figure out what to do next. When you do that, you are working on strategy and thinking," says the parent.

"Should I be thinking about a bad shot or good shot?" asks the child.

"Well, we must look at where we are. Focus on the present and focus on your next shot. It's hard to do, but don't worry about where the ball goes. You have to learn to focus on things that you can control. The one thing you can control is yourself."

"Oh, that's why my older brother got in trouble for not cleaning up his room, but I did clean up my room and I did not get into trouble!" says the child.

"Correct! Why don't we make it a goal for you to go out one afternoon each week and just play a few holes. Play as many or few as you want really, but you must do it concentrating on what you are thinking and not where the ball goes. Alright?" asks the parent.

"Ok. I could play 16, then 13, 14, and 15 if the weather wasn't looking good. Or, I could play 16, 17, 18, 1, 2, and 3! Or, I could start on four and play all nine holes right back to number three!" says the child.

"Right! You got it! Now, what is also really important to scoring?" asks the parent.

"Hitting the ball!" exclaims the child.

"Yes, it is. But chipping and putting are really your best weapons. Just look at Tiger Woods or Luke Donald or Lee Westwood. Sure, they hit the ball great, but they really carve off the shots with the short game. One day per week, you will practice chipping and putting okay?" asks the parent.

"Yeah. I remember that putt Tiger made at the US Open on the last hole. That was cool," says the child.

"To accomplish your goals of winning a local tournament and one of your performance goals of shooting 38 how much time do you think you need to spend chipping and putting?" asks the parent.

"Maybe an hour?" asks the child.

"That sounds reasonable, but only if you are getting something out of that hour," says the parent.

"And not just banging balls around the green like my friend Leon does," says the child.

"Exactly. Have you ever watched Mr. Tim practice? He practices getting the ball up and down. He will take one ball, his putter, and a wedge to the green and practice hitting the chip and making the putt. Do you think that is something you could do?" asks the parent.

"For an hour. One day a week. Yes," says the child.

"Great. Well your second process goal is to practice chipping and putting with one ball one hour each week. Now how about your full swing? What do you think you need to work on?"

"Well the last lesson Mr. Wilkes gave me was on ball position. He wanted me to put some sticks down on the ground," says the child.

"Great. Well why don't you practice your ball position for one hour on the range on your third day? Instead of hitting the same club why don't you go through your whole bag and aim at different targets? Maybe you could hit four shots with every club or something like that," says the parent.

"I can do that," says the child.

"But the sticks must be laid down, right?" asks the parent.

"Right. Because if they are not, I may get confused and start doing something else," says the child.

"Great. We have a plan," says the parent. "Each week you are going to work on your ball position for an hour. Second, each week you are going to chip and putt with one ball for one hour. Third, you are going to go out and play focusing on yourself one day each week. Does that sound like a good plan for you to accomplish your goal of winning a local tournament, and a good way to earn some ice cream by accomplishing your performance goals?"

"Yes sir," answers the child.

"Well we are going to tape these weekly goals to the refrigerator. Each week, it is your responsibility to accomplish these goals. After a month of doing them, I will make sure we get you a lesson and you are heading in the right direction. Okay?" asks the parent.

"Alright!" exclaims the child.

Now which child has a better chance? Go back to the above examples. Go back and think about when things began to go wrong or right. Go back and think about how the plan changed or altered course a bit. Go back and figure out how that fun- loving kid who was interested in golf is now losing his passion. Go back and figure out how that fun- loving kid is now on the PGA Tour. Individually, as a parent, as a country, or as a culture we have only one shot at this. Let's do it the very best we can.

I caution you not to play any blame games here. Everything in this book is reversible. Everything in this book can also be layered a little deeper. It is not "your" fault or "the instructor's" fault. Just tweak your process a bit. The **intention** will always be to win, but the **emphasis** can't be put there during development. Use the years of wisdom in the book to create your own plan. Put some rules in that you, your children, and your family, can be held accountable for accomplishing.

In closing I suggest this: Know Who is in control of your heart before you put your time there. Put your time where your heart is and grade your success carefully.

Oh yeah.... make sure you listen to great music too! Especially Dexter Gordon and Pearl Jam.

V.J. Trolio began instructing and coaching golf in 1999. He became a PGA member in May of 2007 and serves as a teaching professional at Old Waverly Golf in West Point, MS. Old Waverly has been the host to the 1999 USGA Women's Open, 2006 USGA Women's Mid-Amateur and the USGA Women's Amateur in 2019.

Trolio's awards include:
- Golf Magazine Top 100 Teachers in America '14 - '18
- Golf Digest Best in State '16 -'18
- PGA Gulf States Teacher of the Year '08,'10,'17
- PGA Gulf States Player Development Award '15,'16
- PGA Gulf States Junior Golf Leader '11,'13
- Golf Digest Best Young Instructors in America '10 -'12

As a player Trolio graduated from The University of Southern Mississippi, where he was the first in the school's history to qualify for NCAA post season play as an individual. Trolio would win three section Assistant's Championships, '07 Mississippi State Open, and finish runner up in the '03 PGA Assistant National Championship.

As a coach, players on the prestigious Palmer Cup Team, Curtis Cup Team, and PGA Jr. Ryder Cup team were instructed by Trolio.

Jim Gallagher Jr, played a full schedule on the PGA Tour from '84 to '00. He played a full schedule on the PGA Champions Tour from '11 to '14. His father, a PGA club professional and teacher, introduced the game to him at age six. Gallagher would turn professional in '83 after winning both the Indiana State Amateur and State Open in the same year.

Gallagher won five events on the PGA Tour. He was a member of the victorious 1993 Ryder Cup team and the victorious 1994 President Cup Team. He was elected to the University of Tennessee Athletic Hall of Fame in '18.

Elite, competitive, gritty, healthy competitors are made; they are not managed into existence. Tomorrow's generation of athletes will be made primarily by the good judgment and keen discrimination of parents, mentors, and coaches. None of these will be more important than the wisdom of the home.

Time and patience are the two primary ingredients of wisdom. Inside these pages you will find a coach of young athletes in golf for the past twenty years. He will give you researched facts the he applies to young athletes and their teams. The secret is to recognize the difference between intention and emphasis and how to apply it appropriately and consistently. You will also find the untold story of one young athlete that grew into a five-time champion on the PGA Tour and a Ryder Cup hero. You will be able to see behind the curtain of a world-class career and the important role played by those that surround and nurture the athlete. These two, a coach and an athlete, do not wish to persuade you; but instead they wish to push you to think.

This is more than a great story or entertaining read. It is an approach, a mindset, and a guide that you will use to define, create, and apply to your young athlete. All heroes need a guide and sometimes that guide has ONLY ONE SHOT. This book is dedicated to you, the guide.

www.ingramcontent.com/pod-product-compliance
Lightning Source LLC
Chambersburg PA
CBHW070733160426
43192CB00009B/1416